# Dark Ops

# An Anonymous Story

## Written By: Commander X

Legion Sec Multimedia Unit
Montreal, Quebec - CANADA

**Dark Ops: An Anonymous Story**

**First Edition - Paperback**

Published By: Lulu

www.lulu.com

Printed In: USA / UK / EU / CANADA / AUSTRALIA

**ISBN:** 978-1-387-06844-9

# Dedication:

This book is dedicated to one of the greatest heroes Anonymous has ever known, Jeremy Hammond. Despite serving a crushing ten year sentence in the USA, he remains as defiant and non-compliant as the day he was arrested. A brilliant Anarchist, consumate street activist, and an epic part of the idea called Anonymous - Jeremy Hammond is one of those rare individuals who becomes a legend while he is still alive.

www.FreeJeremy.net

•  •  •

# Contents

# INTRODUCTION

*"Light thinks it travels faster than anything but it is wrong. No matter how fast light travels, it finds the darkness has always got there first, and is waiting for it."* ~~ Terry Pratchett

Welcome to *Dark Ops: An Anonymous Story*, which is the sequel to my first book released last year entitled *Behind The Mask: An Inside Look At Anonymous*. In this book I hope to continue the story I began in my prior work. I would like to thank all the readers who made my first book such an amazing success. I hope this satisfies your curiosity about what happened next.

Having successfully escaped from the USA into Canada, the story in *Behind The Mask* leaves off at the triumphal moment after the world premier of the full-length major motion picture documentary *We Are Legion: The Story Of The Hacktivists* in Toronto. And the narrative in this sequel will be similar, but with major differences. There will be noticeably fewer "action" scenes, for the simple reason that there simply wasn't a lot of that sort of thing. While I've continued to be cautious and live in hiding while in exile, the simple fact is that Canada is both unable and unwilling to manhunt me with the same resources that the government of the USA can deploy on its own soil.

As I left the theater that night, feeling a bit like a rock star - I admit to being extremely optimistic about the future of Anonymous. I guess I was naive in that I felt like we had achieved enough power that we would easily be able to handle the growing number of enemies lining up to take shots at us. Part of how wrong I was is attributable to the fact that I honestly believed there were horrors that the USA and *Five-Eyes Nations* were unwilling to perpetrate upon their own citizens in order to quell dissent. It would not be until the Snowden leaks that I would fully realize to what lengths the USA was both capable and willing to go against the Information

Activists. To talk about droning hackers and turning them into pink mist is one thing, but to *actually* do that?

And so this is why I named this book as I did. Because far from Anonymous entering a golden age after November 2012, it instead entered a period so dark and foreboding that it has permanently altered my psyche. I was not born to be a warrior. I am not equipped to have adrenaline flowing through my veins in fight or flight state for years on end. And I certainly am not in any way "fearless", as the readers of my last book can attest. They say that rebellions are built on hope, and that's a good thing - because soon hope is all any of us would have to cling to. In the war between Anonymous and the USA, neither side was going to back down or relent. And both sides would score horrible hits against the other.

And it wasn't just the USA, NATO and the Five-Eyes Nations. Anonymous was about to take on other extremely powerful and dangerous enemies. The Vatican, Israel, The "King" of Bahrain, and pretty much *all* of the police in the West. These are relentless and brutal adversaries, capable of any horror you can imagine. And like us, they never forget and they never forgive. The days of easy victories over weakened dictators that made for such dramatic scenes on the big screen were over. The Transnational Global Cyber Insurgency truly came into being, and the *Dark Ops* had begun. The hackers and *Anonymous* had become the last line of defense for a world on the brink of extinction.

www.CommanderX.info

Commander X - January 3, 2017 - Amesbury, Ontario - Canada

# ONE

## *Operation Vendetta*
------------------------

*"But when a long train of abuses and usurpations, pursuing invariably the same Object evinces a design to reduce them under absolute Despotism, it is their right, it is their duty, to throw off such Government, and to provide new Guards for their future security."*

~~ US Declaration Of Independence

Tuesday - November 6, 2012 approx. 6:00 PM ET  - Starbucks Toronto, Ontario - CANADA

There have been very few hacks that I have participated in that made me even slightly nervous, much less terrified. Usually I was at the most anxious to see if it would work. But this hack....this was more outrageous than anything we had ever contemplated, and I was actually sweating like a pig. Because tonight my *Crew* and I had hacked into the national election in the USA. No, seriously.

It had begun roughly a year and a half ago. I was sitting in a McDonalds in San Francisco late one night chatting with my *Crew* about what additional attacks we could launch as part of *Operation Vendetta*. Even during those initial brain-storming sessions I remember feeling insane trepidation at what we were contemplating. It was the only hack in my life I remember hoping that it would fail, that we wouldn't be able to do it. But we did do it. We were doing it.

The manifesto for the hack was simple: to find any way we could to destabilize and de-legitimize the 2012 national election in the USA. It was an apolitical approach, we would not attempt to favor either candidate. In fact we would take pains not to. Instead the goal we settled on was in showing how easily we hacked in, doing some random damage - and then putting out a statement after detailing the hacks and pointing out the obvious fact that if we could do it, others probably also did too. This line of argument ultimately leading to - no one actually knows who did win the national election in the USA. And whomever they crown would be thus de-legitimized by those lingering questions, and the entire democratic process in the USA would be brought into question over the doubts whether it could ever be secured from network hacking attempts.

It was my core inner *Crew* that made the pact. And we spent a year and a half preparing. Unfortunately, hacks like this don't happen in convenient ten minute segments between ads for sneakers and breakfast cereal like on "Mr. Robot".

We began simply enough, I spent days researching white papers and YouTube videos on proof-of-concept hacks against everything from individual voting machines to the ORCA electronic vote counting systems. The latter ended up as our primary attack vector for Florida and Ohio. In addition, we worked up two voting machine hacks. One involved inserting a thumb drive into a particular model stupid enough to have a USB port exposed, and the other was even simpler - literally involving simply placing a powerful magnet in a certain location on the machine. These "machine hacks" we then packaged up along with a brief manifesto and quietly spread them among the underground, encouraging people to go out and randomly apply the procedures in their own voting stations on election day.

And it was not smooth sailing. After months of work on this, one of the six people in my Crew turned out to be a snitch working as a Confidential Informant for the FBI. He had been privy to all the initial brainstorming sessions, and knew enough to cause the FBI to take serious notice. There was actually a robust debate within the Crew when Locke's deception came to light. Consideration was given to dropping the attempt. But Locke had been outed before we got access to the ORCA systems, he only knew for certain about the voting machine hacks we were slowly spreading within the underground. Which is why when he got desperate to give his handlers something, Locke actually came back to our Crew IRC and attempted to get back into our graces with none other than a "stolen" voting machine - one no doubt given to him by the FBI to try and get back into the Crew. This is from the actual IRC log, one of the handful I have ever kept.

Locke: Commandant. Commander X, I've been waiting for like 5 stinkin' hours.

Commander X: Indeed. And why would you be waiting so long?

Locke: Because I freakin' love tea.

*Author's Note*: This was Locke's old recognition phrase, only he and I knew it.

Commander X: Indeed, so I have been told. I would suggest Starbucks next time, they have excellent tea. Or latte. Beats waiting in an IRC for five hours.

Locke: Why didn't you run when I told you to.

Commander X: As you may recall, I was sick. Very sick.

Locke: PM

Commander X: I see the PM. Anything you have to say to me you can say to the entire Crew, who you also betrayed.

Locke: Well if that's the welcome that's here, we really don't need you. You just have an eloquent way of saying things.

Commander X: YOU don't need ME? This is MY channel, it's the other way around. And we have been doing just fine lately. Despite your treachery. As I recall our last conversation, you were done with the PLF and me.

Locke: Because I said go and all of a sudden you're pinched.

Commander X: Actually you said you talked to the feds and told them I was in Orlando on my way north. I do not recall any warning, or indication I should run. What I DO recall is I also transmitted to you my exact address, the very address where the following day I was mysteriously arrested by 6 FBI agents. That is my recollection.

Locke: Your address?

You never told me your address. That's definitely not something you would have given me.

Commander X: Yes, I certainly did. It was necessary for you in order to wire me money. Which was the point of the conversation we had last time we spoke.

I used the coffee house address. The same coffee house where the very next day I was arrested by federal agents.

Locke: Which was great until men in expensive clothing come to my school and bother me while I'm in fucking class. If you think I fucking pinched you, you've got another thing coming. I had no idea where you were. I knew you were in SF. I knew where money was supposed to go. That's it.

Commander X: What I am saying is, that's quite a coincidence - from my point of view you understand.

Locke: I do understand. But I seriously jumped on IRC after I could get somewhere that wasn't at school and told you what happened ASAP. I still get fucking emails from the FBI about anon shit. You think I want that kind of attention?

Commander X: Yes, you said you had a conversation with the feds and told them false info. Here's my question, why even do that much? Why didn't you tell them to go fuck themselves? That's what I do when ever I get V&ed. I give them the finger with one hand, and my lawyers card with the other. Why talk to them at all? Why EVER talk to them, for any reason?

Locke: Because it made sense for you to be in Orlando. They thought you were in fucking Orlando. Because I don't have a choice.

Commander X: No they didn't think I was in Orlando.

Locke: You said so yourself they thought you were in Orlando.

Commander X: Bullshit. We all have choices. I have never said one fucking word to the bastards. And I have much more to lose than you, I have indictments that add up to 35 years in prison. And if as you say you have no choice, then how can one assume you are not even now helping them by logging this conversation?

Locke: Why the fuck do you think I would come back. Deal with this which I knew was going to happen.

Commander X: Because they are very pissed that I escaped into exile in Canada. Because they would like very much to re-capture me. That is why you would so suddenly pop up. Perhaps like our friend Sabu, you got pinched. And now you are working off your debt to them.

YDT10: They are such unhappy people. No wonder why Locke seems so unhappy :(

Commander X: They are indeed.

Locke: Whatever man. They don't own me, I got off scot free because I wasn't dumb enough to DDoS from my house. Or targets inside of the US.

Commander X: Ah so you DID get busted then? You must have neglected to tell me that when I was giving you my address. The day before I got V&ed.

Locke: They show up at my school, I'd say I was pretty well busted.

I TOLD YOU TO GO YOU DUMB MOTHER. I SAID GTFO of dodge.

Commander X: No, you told me you misdirected them. Essentially telling me I was safe.

Locke: If I ratted you, why say anything to you. Your capture would be good for me. IF they were on me now. Why would I identify myself. Why not start over?

Commander X: Because I have very PUBLICLY entered exile in Canada and given them the finger. Because they are mad and want me, that's why Locke.

Locke: You think they give a fuck that you're in Canada? Jurisdiction doesn't mean fucking shit.

YDT10: LOL

Commander X: Yes they do. I have given interviews to CNN, Greek TV and NBC. Basically saying fuck you. And now another of the Anonymous 16 has followed my example and bolted. That makes them very mad Locke, and they would easily make you do this to try and draw me out.

YDT10: Bad role model Commander X. How can I look up to you if you're going to make me into a bad person?

Locke: Meh, if I wanted to draw you out I would befriend you differently. Not tell you who I am.

YDT10: Locke why are you such an unhappy person? :( Does it hurt to be a failure? Is that why you're so unhappy?

Locke: I'm not unhappy YDT10, I suggest staying quiet, X can handle himself.

Commander X: Maybe you have? And since that failed, you tried this instead. See Locke, I am not easy to befriend like that anymore. I have learned much from getting V&ed. Including who I can and can not trust.

Locke: Ah cool, well here's the dealio. I'm about to pull off something fucking funny but I need this guys magic voice to make it happen. I'm stealing a voting machine.

Commander X: Good for you. Good luck with that.

Locke: I need you to get me somebody to reverse engineer it.

Poppy: O-o

Commander X: That won't happen Locke, and FYI this channel is almost certainly monitored by the feds.

Locke: Who cares. Everything is monitored. They don't even need a warrant. Wiretap? Nah, they have that shit tagged and searchable somewhere.

Commander X: Sabu knew that too, and yet he blabbed all over. But then he had nothing to fear, as he worked for them. :-D

Locke: Lulzsec was/is/and always will be a joke. 54 days of look at us, then it got hot and they're like fuq dis no lulz 4 us.

Commander X: So let me get this straight, you Mr paranoid himself - and now you think it's fine to talk about stealing voting machines in a public channel guaranteed to be monitored?

Locke: Sure, they can't find me. I have no name here where I am.

Commander X: Yeah, right. Or maybe, because you work for them you can say whatever you want to and you're safe. Hell Locke, you can even commit crimes like Sabu did and you can't be prosecuted.

Locke: The part I'm missing. Is if I can get away with committing crimes. Why identify myself? If I had the feds working with me, why not start over, put out some good work and get rep from Anon?

Commander X: Perhaps you could do that. Or you could try and tempt me by stealing a voting machine. The Locke I knew would long ago have told us all to fuck off and left, why so persistent - will your handlers be pissed at you if you fail to gain my trust again? Either strategy will fail, as I said I don't give my trust easily anymore. And either way, you would as an informant be free to act with impunity as you can not be prosecuted.

Commander X: Yep, so now you all know how I got vanned. And you just met the snitch who did it to me. I can't fucking stand snitches. Wonder which two users there are the fed handler?

----------

After this conversation took place, the paranoia level of the Crew went through the roof. It is the greatest wonder to me that any of us found the courage to actually continue with the strike after Locke snitched. Especially with Sabu having so recently and famously brought down LulzSec and AntiSec by becoming himself a CI for the FBI.

But the fact is we did continue the work, and it had all....even Locke's treachery, it had all led to this fateful night.

The five remaining members of the Crew had gathered in a new encrypted platform we had just started using called Jabber with OTR. Our plan was to watch the media reports coming in throughout the evening, and see if events opened up any interesting opportunities. We had continuous access to the vote counting systems in both Ohio and Florida. Eventually if nothing else happened our plan called for depositing a simple virus that would begin slowly gobbling up vote counts totally at random and then leave those systems. Eventually the plan called for us to put out a press release and reveal the code for the virus, which systems we put it in, and the proof-of-concept voting machine hacks as well. But like so many well-laid plans, it just wasn't to be....

Vect0r: Ermmm, guys.... I think we have a problem.

Commander X: No. No problems. Not tonight. What fucking problems?

Vect0r: Whelp. We're not alone in Ohio or Florida.

Gh0stAn0n: What the fuck does that even mean?

Commander X: Vect0r, explain - what are you seeing in there?

Vect0r: There's another crew inside both systems. And if I am reading this right, they are also in a few we aren't in. Pennsylvania, Michigan, I see tunnels leading off everywhere really.

PizzaMan: Jesus. Who is it? Can you tell?

Vect0r: I'm running a backtrace now, should have some info in a few moments.

Commander X: Any signs they have seen us? Do they know were in there with them?

Vext0r: No, at least I don't think so anyway.

DigitalTerrorist: Great. Just fucking great. So what do we do now?

Vect0r: I don't know, but hold onto your seats folks because I just geo-located the IPs of the attackers and you are not going to believe this. They all point to the Ohio State Headquarters of the Republican Party. And I am not even joking.

Commander X: Jesus fucking christ....the GOP?

Gh0stAn0n: It's obvious what they are trying to do. Karl Rove took over the entire Ohio State headquarters this morning. I knew they had a plan like this. I told you guys.

Commander X: It is? Enlighten us. What "plan" do they have?

Gh0stAn0n: Well, it looks like Obama will take the election by at least a couple of million votes, right? So if you want to change the outcome, you either have to mess with a fuck lot of popular votes that need to be changed, or....mess with the Electoral College instead. Bust into battleground States, and delete just a few votes in hundreds of districts. The math works, you can steal an election that way - I explained this to you all before. You'd use a virus just like ours actually.

VectOr: Wow. I never would have thought of that, even seeing everything I saw. It makes total sense though. That is brilliant.

DigitalTerrorist: The question is, what do we do now?

Commander X: Nothing. This changes nothing. We came here to sow chaos, and we are sticking to the plan.

PizzaMan: Wait a minute. No offense X, but we all worked hard on this for over a year. I think we should consider our options and discuss this. I mean, that is why we agreed to wait until election night anyway, to see if anything interesting developed. This seems....interesting.

VectOr: What are you thinking Pizza?

PizzaMan: Well, your the man with the foot in the door in these systems, do you think we can, I don't know - throw the Republicans out of the systems?

Commander X: To what fucking end? "Save the election for Obama" and become "heroes" of American Democracy?

PizzaMan: Well, all the over the top hyperbole aside, yeah something like that I guess.

VectOr: I can lock them out of Ohio and Florida. I am not sure if I can kick them out of the other States, we don't have root there. However it might be possible to trip the security in those systems alerting them to the GOP presence on their servers. Snitch them out.

DigitalTerrorist: I don't know, I'm with X I think on this one. I don't believe in either of these bozos I don't want to save shit for anyone. We came here to wreck it, let's wreck it.

VectOr: One thing to consider, if we do this - kick out the Repubs and announce we saved the election for Obama, we will be looked on as heroes. Anonymous could use the help with our reputation as of late.

DigitalTerrorist: I thought we were doing this under our Crew flag, the PLF?

Commander X: We were. But no way we are doing this shit, saving the election - under *my* Crew's flag. I draw the line there.

PizzaMan: So you'll go with the idea of kicking out the GOP X?

Commander X: I'll reluctantly and with great reservations go with whatever the Crew wants to go with. Just saying, you'll need to invent a sock to put that shit out, it's not going out on our label, no way.

VectOr: We can call ourselves "The Protectors". Say we're a patriot crew in Anonymous.

PizzaMan: I love it!

Commander X: OMG you guys are *such* dorks.

And that's how we went, in ten short minutes - from wrecking the US Election of 2012 to quite possibly saving it for Obama against GOP meddling. Later that night, as Karl Rove was giving what amounted to his victory speech for the Republican Presidential candidate, someone came up and whispered in his ear and he went spit flying ballistic on live television.

While we'll never know, I would like to think it was at that very moment that an aid told him the hackers he sent in had been booted.

Days later we packaged the whole thing up and sent it to the media. We invented a Crew in Anonymous called the *Protectors of Democracy* (a name that still makes me want to vomit), gathered what little forensic evidence we had on the GOP, and blasted the entire thing to the world's media outlets. To their credit, several had the balls to actually go with the story. In the underground, the whole thing became a bit of a legend. Anonymous has been credited with many amazing things but saving the election for Barack Obama has to be right up there near the top of the "most epic list". Sort of ironic since Obama has tormented, tortured, jailed and even killed more Information Activists in his eight years than all other previous Presidents combined. Hell of a way to show your gratitude.

But it wasn't what we set out to do. And I still believe it was the wrong choice. The original manifesto for the hack, the concept of destabilizing and delegitimizing elections in the USA - would continue to resonate and grow within the underground. And four years hence, this strategy would resurface in the Resistance with a vengeance. And this time, there would be no saving anything for anyone.

Several months later, the hacker I have called "Vect0r" live tweeted as he went out on Golden Gate Bridge and threw the laptop he had done the election hack with into the San Francisco Bay. He then left the *Underground*, got a good paying job as a White Hat security consultant - and never looked back. It was that sort of hack.

*Author's Note*: In light of the extraordinary events unfolding in our world as I begin writing the story in *Dark Ops: An Anonymous Story,* it seems incumbent upon me to at least comment on election hacking in general, and the specific incidents surrounding the National Election of 2016 in the USA.

The first question many have is: how hard is it to actually hack the elections in the USA? The answer is, it's really easy. From affecting the individual machines, to kicking in the back doors to the State and regional counting systems - it was far from the most difficult hack I have ever participated in. The simple fact is taken as a whole, elections in the USA may well be the single most target rich surface in all of Black Hat hacking. With 50 sovereign States having their own systems, and even differences between districts within those States - there is simply no way to secure such a hodge-podge of software and hardware. This is exasperated by the fact that all this equipment and software is commercial and closed source.

As for so-called "State Actors", my Crew saw no evidence of this in 2012. I have likewise seen no convincing evidence that such was a measurable factor in 2016. The fact remains that the *only* actors I know for certain ever hacked an election in the USA was my Crew and the GOP led by Karl Rove's team of dirty-tricksters. So what do I think happened in 2016?

As both my first book and this one have been at pains to point out, the USA is at war, *real* war - with the Information Activists in the West. From Julian Assange to myself, we have detailed many stories of the brutal persecution of hacktivists by the government of the USA. It is my opinion that a concerted and massive campaign, led by Julian Assange and WikiLeaks, and consisting of thousands of Information Activists around the world - is what caused the "disruption" in the national election of the USA in 2016.

Whether or not some small part of the leaked material that fueled this massive propaganda campaign against the stability and legitimacy of the elections in the USA came from agents of the Russian government or not is immaterial. The material leaked itself proves that what cost the DNC its victory was an almost comically flawed campaign strategy, and not the *Russians*. So bottom line, no - the *Russians* didn't do it. We did. The Information Activists of the world.

To my mind this is the ultimate lesson of the fiasco of the national election of 2016 in the USA. That waging war against the world's hackers is insane, and a battle you can not possibly win. It proves once again that information alone if wielded properly can have as great or greater effect on geo-political events than kinetic force does. And it shows that *Truth* can be wielded as a weapon against the corrupt powers of this world.

It bears remembering that leaks of sensitive information can not harm the truly righteous. Such disclosures only damage the corrupt and criminal class. The USA is an Empire built exclusively upon lies, secrets - and corruption. It is therefore no mistake that it is the USA, with the most to lose from our power - that has targeted Information Activists with such brutal persecution. But as the events of 2016 show, the Information Activists, Hackers, and hacktivists - are perfectly capable of wreaking havoc upon anyone who would attempt to silence or harm us. Even the Empire of the USA. The following is a report I wrote after extensively investigating the circumstances of 2016.

----------

Russians, Russians....Everywhere: What Really Happened To The 2016 US Election, Who Did It, & Why

Before we dive into a little reality check for America, I would like to lay out what this article is, and is not – and what you the reader can expect to take away from it. This way you can save time, and simply decide not to read further.

What I am willing to offer you is the Truth as I have discovered it. My quest for this particular Truth began quite sometime prior to even the concept of election hacking, with an investigation into the Guccifer phenomenon.

I did not search out these Truths so that I could enlighten the world, I am not a journalist. This is part of my job as an Information Activist to be aware of the playing field and actors operating in Cyber Space. As such, I neither have, nor would I provide if I did – any sort of hard 'forensic' evidence of what I am about to tell you. For the average reader, the veracity of my conclusions must rest solely upon my own reputation in both knowledge and honesty. I am simply not in the business of providing evidence to the world and potentially law enforcement that could be used against my fellow hackers in the Underground. If it's proof you demand, your journalists and law enforcement will need to seek that out themselves based on what I will present here – as I'll not help them. That is their job, not mine.

What I will provide is a cogent and logical, albeit radically different – concept of what actually took place during the latest election cycle in the USA. It will tangent more than a few data points already in the public domain, more than enough to warrant and facilitate further investigation. Certainly enough to bring into question the prevailing narrative coming from the USA government and its proxy media in the west regarding the latest election. With all this in mind, this is what I learned investigating the circumstances of the 2016 Election in the USA.

As I stated above, my investigation began long before the election cycle in the USA even got underway, and was instead centered on what I have come to call the Guccifer Phenomenon. And here at the very beginning is where I will straight away leave the mainstream narrative behind with a startling discovery. Wrap your mind around this, Guccifer is not a person – it is a Crew! Approximately six to eight individuals from Ukraine, Serbia, and Romania. Now let's drill down on this so you understand exactly what I mean here. First I don't believe this Crew ever called themselves Guccifer Crew.

That was most likely a stage name, not even the actual hacker handle but a simple front name – for the person who was the leader of this Crew. An individual we now know is a Romanian hacker currently serving consecutive terms first in Romania than in the USA for cyber crime related offenses.

Eventually, I made contact with one member of this Crew whom I shall not name. Nor will I share what we discussed in specific terms. We talked in general about the state of hacktivism in the West versus Eastern Europe and Russia. We specifically spoke in that regard about Anonymous and its presence in Russia. I found this individual to be calm and thoughtful, intelligent and skilled. My feeling is that like so many Hacker Crews coming from that region, they didn't even fly a flag or even have a name for their Crew. Certainly, they had no public meme like that. They did seem very tight, loyal, and compatible. While not affiliated with Anonymous, they were in contact with and worked with individual Anons and Anonymous Cells all over the world. A solid underground Crew with no need for glamor, or even a name. And certainly not affiliated with any Nation State. Of this, I'm absolutely certain.

Now let's examine the three major cyber-related events that appear to have significantly influenced the Election, and caused massive chaos in the government of the USA. First, the hack and dump of the DNC E-Mail spool. We all know who everyone says did it, the omnipowerful and omnipresent Russian Spooks. Obviously, my investigation led me to a completely different conclusion. Instead, for me, the trail led to a Cell within the Global Collective called Anonymous Russia. This National Cell is managed by approximately eight individuals, six of whom have been arrested by Russian authorities since the election and charged with some extremely weird cyber-offenses. One member of this Cell managed to escape and is publicly seeking political asylum in Eastern Europe.

I believe this Cell liberated the DNC E-Mail spool, gave it to the Guccifer Crew, who in turn delivered it to WikiLeaks for publication. This hand-off was necessitated not for obfuscation of nation state involvement, but because of the language gap – which the Guccifer Crew is better at navigating than Anonymous Russia.

The motive here was simple political hacktivism. Like it or not Russian Information Activists have as much reason (arguably more) to hate the USA as Jester and his "Patriot Hackers" have to hate Russia. And to argue they were either State sponsored or State sanctioned is ludicrous and ignores the glaring reality that the entire cell was wiped out by FSB, save one lone Anon who escaped – just after the election.

That brings us to the Podesta hack and dump of his personal E-Mail spool. This was accomplished in-house by the Guccifer Crew. And again, this was strictly motivated by political hacktivism, in this case specifically, it was the NATO interference in the Ukraine situation. Which brings us to the persona known publicly as Guccifer 2.0. There has been so much speculation as to this individual. Except....they're not. An individual, that is. This is simply the main public account of the current Guccifer Crew (sans their leader, who's in prison) which I believe is admined by the person who now leads the Crew, but is accessible to at least two other individuals in the Crew. There are numerous leads I can't discuss that led me to this particular conclusion. But one piece of public evidence screams out, and cinched it up for me as a Black Hat hacker myself.

In the course of these events, both Guccifer and Guccifer 2.0 gave interviews to main stream media outlets. It was the first, with the original Guccifer, currently incarcerated in Romania, that I paid the closest attention to in order to determine how legitimate Guccifer 2.0 was. You might ask, how does that work?

Simple. Black Hat hackers are a culture, and quite predictable in many areas. One of those is namespace. Your handle is everything, it's your brand, your personal reputation, and eventually your legacy. Hackers in the Underground are extremely covetous of this namespace. The name Guccifer is a truly fantastic namespace, both topically because it just sounds cool and is easy to remember, and also because of the legacy the first original Guccifer attached to it with his amazing hacks. If Guccifer 2.0 were anything but 100% legitimate, the original Guccifer would have made an unmistakable point in no uncertain terms of outing and denying the persona during his interview. Instead, he did exactly the opposite, not saying one word about Guccifer 2.0. Because they were his Crew. Guccifer didn't cooperate when captured, he remained loyal to his Crew and would do anything to protect them. This is all obvious and beyond dispute to actual Black Hat Hackers in the Underground, who understand that honor is everything and that collaborators should rot in hell.

This brings us to WikiLeaks. Some have tried to argue that these dumps could have been accomplished without the assistance of WikiLeaks. This is plain stupid. Yes, there are many disclosure platforms that have cropped up in WikiLeaks wake – but to have the sort of devastating political impact that these disclosures had requires the top shelf, not spin-offs. The expertise and sheer grace with which Julian navigated these bombshell disclosures once again affirms his utter genius in the realm of Information Activism.

There has been a massive attempt by the disingenuous msm media in the West to try to somehow connect WikiLeaks to the Russian government, thus explaining the motivation for his disclosure strategy. Now, I'm not going to attempt to speak for or climb into the head of Julian Assange, despite my deep love for him and the mutual respect we share as comrades in this movement. But I am going to state some obvious and well-known facts.

WikiLeaks and Anonymous, as well as the Hacker Underground in the West – are at war with the government of the USA. This war was declared by the USDOJ in 2010, and has been raging ever since. This is well-established hacktivist history.

While no other motivation is necessary to adequately explain the actions of WikiLeaks in this election, there is another motivation I suspect crossed Assange's mind. I know for a fact that for many years Julian's over-arching concern has been obtaining the freedom of alleged leaker Chelsea Manning from her 35 year prison term. Her commutation was so controversial, so politically charged, that I believe Obama would have used any excuse he could find to avoid it. Had Hillary won the election, her being a fellow liberal may have been enough for Obama to say fuck it and punt the whole mess into her term for her to deal with. And come on, as much as Clinton despises WikiLeaks and Julian do you really believe she would have ever helped Manning? I for one seriously doubt it. That would have meant at bare minimum Chelsea would have remained in a cage for an additional twelve to sixteen years awaiting a new pardon cycle with a new liberal leadership. And if that didn't come, she may well have served the entire sentence – if she survived. Trump getting elected forced Obama's hand, and left him with little choice but to do the right thing.

Tandem to WikiLeaks actions during the election, there were a handful of Anons and Information Activists here in the west (myself included) who seeing this successful strategy unfolding leaped in to assist WikiLeaks in the dissemination of the disclosures, and to generally support the effort by wreaking havoc in any way possible. This group was small, maybe eight individuals – as most of the western Information Activists didn't understand the point and thought Julian had gone crazy or been co-opted by the Russians.

And like everyone else we've examined so far, and particularly co-tangent to WikiLeaks – the motivation of this small band of hacktivists assisting Wikileaks was hatred of the USA for its political persecution of Information Activists using the brutal CFAA.

There has been much talk from the western White Hats about signatures. The Russian Spooks did it, because the IP address signature, the code signature, and the behavioral signatures all matched a supposed gang of Russian Agents hacking for the State. Let's start with the IP signatures. Please. It's called a VPN. Mine has three Russian exit nodes if I need them. Then there's always IP spoofing. An IP is zero evidence of anything, and anyone who is honest needs to admit this. As for code signatures, this may impress the average citizen – but a Black Hat will simply laugh out loud. We trade, sell, and steal each others code (and code from White Hats as well) so much that this is a ridiculous thing to try and pin down. I just busted open a random script for a payload I have in my arsenal and I counted code from five countries on three continents in one package.

That leaves behavioral signatures. In the above analysis of the Election, there were essentially only two primary hacks involved, the DNC and Podesta attacks. They were both simple E-Mail spool theft and dump operations. Something the Russian Intelligence has never done in its entire history. But there is a group for whom E-Mail hack and dump is a very signature behavior: Anonymous. Let's look at some recent history.

2008: Sarah Palin's E-Mail is hacked by Anonymous and her spool is dumped to WikiLeaks, who published them.

2010: HB Gary Federal, a cyber security contractor – is hacked by Anonymous. Seventy thousand E-Mails are taken and published on Barrett Brown's site Project PM.

2011: A hacktivist crew loosely affiliated with Anonymous called Anti Sec hacks the private Intelligence firm Stratfor, stealing years of E-Mail and eventually dumping them to WikiLeaks who published them as the "Global Intelligence Files".

2012: My own Crew, together with Anti Sec – hack the E-Mail of the entire Syrian government, including the private accounts of President Assad and his wife. In total, over 70 million E-Mails are liberated, dumped to WikiLeaks, and were subsequently published.

How's that for signature behavior?  O-o You know what they said to Cinderella, right?  If the shoe fits....

This brings us to the final cyber phenomenon of the 2016 Election in the USA, the propaganda war. This is the one and only thing blamed on the Russians in which their government most likely had a hand. During all modern elections in the West, Russia has run a clumsy and awkward (and not terribly effective) online propaganda campaign aligned to their interests. They use a combination of so-called "fake news" posts generated in massive spam-like waves using easily obtainable software, and thousands of sock troll accounts on social media. Some of these socks are managed by paid trolls, others are run by government agents using software like Metal Gear designed to allow one person to control numerous online personas.

These campaigns are standard OP for Russian Intelligence, and are massive and quite expensive to run. They are also normally quite useless at having any effect at all on the target demographic, and are usually not even noticed by the general public. It is only the extremely unusual circumstances of this US election cycle that caused this ubiquitous Russian effort to gain some small traction and attention this time.

It is the only direct intervention by the Russian State into the US election cycle in 2016, and I intend to dismiss it henceforth from this analysis simply because while it finally got noticed this time around, the shit simply doesn't work. I have no idea why the Russians continue to pour money into these online troll propaganda campaigns, but they just do not work.

In conclusion, my investigation – unprecedented in that it was carried out from inside the Black Hat Underground culture, has determined that there was in fact a concerted effort to weaponize Trump by getting him elected. This was done so that he would sow chaos and discord within the Federal Government of the USA, with the over-arching goal of punishing it for its treatment of dissenters and Information Activists – and to lessen its ability to project its power globally and harm innocents. And while this goal may be something the Russian government also desires, and while they may have caught on and jumped on the coat-tails of this effort with a clumsy and ineffective propaganda campaign, the idea was not theirs, was certainly not directed by them – and in the end their contribution to this strike was minimal.

Rather the actions that led to Trump being elected and the ensuing mayhem within and damage to the government of the USA was carried out by a disparate and only loosely organized band of approximately 30 Information Activists from around the world, led by Julian Assange, whose interests coincidentally aligned, and who were reasonably lucky in their strategy. As discussed above this band included the Guccifer Crew, Anonymous Russia, WikiLeaks, and a handful of western Information Activists who chose to fly no flag for this action.

The results achieved in this strike were beyond even our most optimistic hopes.

The Federal government is now essentially an Ouroboros, eating itself alive. Massive questions are being asked about the "deep state" comprised of the CIA/NSA/FBI surveillance complex. In fact, the White House has now been pitted directly against these evil entities thanks to the follow-up publication of the CIA Vault 7 WikiLeaks disclosures. The USA's ability to project geopolitical power has been severely compromised by the lack of trust that even allied and friendly nations usually have for the USA. Unprecedented doubt has been thrown upon the so-called "American Democracy", especially in its ability to have fair and free elections. And finally, Chelsea Manning will be released in May. A pretty astounding success for a few dozen hacktivists with laptops, working around the world to fight this Empire of the USA. And we did it without any help or direction from the non-existent Russian Spooks. This is the power of Information Activism. This is the power of the hacktivist. This is how Information Activism will do more in the next decade to make our world a more just and free place for humans than any movement in human history.

*Post Script: I reiterate here the offer I have made publicly in recent months, to both the USA and Russian governments. I will gladly return to the USA in order to offer testimony and evidence to Congress regarding the election in the USA, the above report – and how to end the war between the world's Black Hat hackers and the government of the USA by ceasing political persecution of Information Activists and reforming the CFAA. I will only give testimony to Congress or directly in person to President Trump, and I will never debrief either the FBI or the CIA. I will require in advance a full Presidential Pardon, and a guarantee of Full Immunity when I testify.*

*The counter proposal is addressed to the Russian Government. I will happily travel to Moscow and testify under oath in the Duma regarding the details of the above report. The Russian people, and their government – have been so brutally maligned in the West that I feel they deserve to hear the Truth from someone who is actually on the inside of the Hacker Underground. I will require full and permanent political asylum and transport from Canada to Russia.*

# TWO

## *Operation Israel*
--------------------

*"If the government shuts down your Internet,
shut down your government."*

~~ Anonymous Egypt

Thursday - November 15, 2012 approx. 12:15 AM ET - "Safe House"
Fredericton, New Brunswick - CANADA

The early North Easter had struck New Brunswick with a sudden fury
that didn't surprise me. I was after all, born and raised right next door
in the State of Maine. But nothing had prepared me for the brutal
Maritimes winter. I had fled the Toronto winter to the comfort of a
"safe house" owned by none other than OpNoPro, who some of my
readers may remember from my first book. From the moment of my
arrival, OpNopro and I had happily been turning his living room into
an Anonymous Command Center. With the two oldest known Anons
under one roof, we were both delighted at the prospect of setting up to
cause as much coordinated trouble as possible while I was visiting.

Both OpNoPro and I were night owls by nature. We tended to stay
up all night hacking away and sleep until noon. It was late at night,
and while OpNoPro relaxed watching a movie on his PC, I was in an
IRC chat with a bunch of Anons - some of whom were veterans of the
original *Freedom Operations* in 2011. With no particular Operation
happening, we were sitting around telling the newer Anons old war
stories about the original Freedom Ops. Suddenly someone new
appeared on the server. The person was obviously from the Middle
East, and we would soon learn he was a 15 year old Palestinian living
in Gaza. And he was single-handedly, in less than two minutes - about
to set Anonymous at total war with Israel.

FreePalestine2012: I am a Palestinian in the Gaza Strip. We need the
help of Anonymous. I was told to come here and ask.

Commander X: You can ask. But you should be aware Anonymous is
no one's personal army. There is no guarantee we can help you.

AnonVen0m: Maybe start at the beginning and just tell us what's up FreePalestine2012.

FreePalestine2012: Israel is about to begin a new bombing campaign in Gaza. We can already hear the planes and helicopters above us. And a few minutes ago they dropped flyers warning they were going to turn off the Internet in Gaza.

Commander X: Well fuck me....

CosmoKid: Pics or it didn't happen kid. Snap a shot of the flyer and upload it.

FreePalestine2012: Already done, here's the link. --> CLICK HERE

AnonVen0m: It legit says they're going to shut off the Internet. Fuckers....

There was almost a half minute of silence in the IRC as everyone absorbed both the news, and the uncanny fact that it came during a discussion about the original Freedom Ops. But I didn't even hesitate for a moment. I like so many other hackers in the world longed for a reason to go at Israeli cyberspace over their deplorable treatment of the Palestinians. While the others processed the idea, I spent that thirty seconds, no joke - registering the Op Israel Twitter account (@Op_Israel), which persists to this day. I knew the moment to hold Israel to account had finally arrived. I had already been in too many of these epic and historic moments not to realize this.

Then in a furious and synchronized way that Anonymous is occasionally capable of working, the entire IRC channel burst into action according to a tried and true template called the *Freedom Ops*. First, an encrypted collaborative pad was set up so that some of us could quickly draft a press release on behalf of Anonymous.

A URL was registered and a website set up almost immediately. Within two hours of the young Palestinian's visit, the media was already writing about us, and bombs were already falling on Gaza. And one of the single most titanic cyber conflicts in history was engaged. The first media reports mentioning Anonymous were out in hours, and before any of us got any sleep that night it was dozens of reports and the Twitter account had seven thousand followers! The high-impact video was breath-taking, and followed the general script of the press release - which had become customary in these Ops.

----------

Anonymous Operation Israel - Press Release

Thursday - November 15, 2012 2:00 AM ET USA

Greetings World --

For far too long, Anonymous has stood by with the rest of the world and watched in despair the barbaric, brutal and despicable treatment of the Palestinian people in the so called "Occupied Territories" by the Israel Defense Force. Like so many around the globe, we have felt helpless in the face of such implacable evil. And today's insane attack and threatened invasion of Gaza was more of the same.

But when the government of Israel publicly threatened to sever all Internet and other telecommunications into and out of Gaza they crossed a line in the sand. As the former dictator of Egypt Mubarack learned the hard way - we are ANONYMOUS and NO ONE shuts down the Internet on our watch. To the IDF and government of Israel we issue you this warning only once.

Do NOT shut down the Internet into the "Occupied Territories", and cease and desist from your terror upon the innocent people of Palestine or you will know the full and unbridled wrath of Anonymous. And like all the other evil governments that have faced our rage, you will NOT survive it unscathed.

To the people of Gaza and the "Occupied Territories", know that Anonymous stands with you in this fight. We will do everything in our power to hinder the evil forces of the IDF arrayed against you. We will use all our resources to make certain you stay connected to the Internet and remain able to transmit your experiences to the world. As a start, we have put together the Anonymous Gaza Care Package - http://bit.ly/XH87C5 - which contains instructions in Arabic and English that can aid you in the event the Israel government makes good on its threat to attempt to sever your Internet connection. It also contains useful information on evading IDF surveillance, and some basic first aid and other useful information. We will continue to expand and improve this document in the coming days, and we will transmit it to you by every means at our disposal. We encourage you to download this package, and to share it with your fellow Palestinians to the best of your ability.

We will be with you. No matter how dark it may seem, no matter how alone and abandoned you may feel - know that tens of thousands of us in Anonymous are with you and working tirelessly around the clock to bring you every aid and assistance that we can.

We Are Anonymous

We Are Everywhere

We Are Legion

We Do Not Forgive

We Do Not Forget

To the oppressors of the innocent Palestinian people, it is too late to EXPECT US

-------------------------------------------

Anonymous Global - www.AnonymousGlobal.org

Videos -

http://www.youtube.com/watch?v=UHzMB4vnqW8

http://www.youtube.com/watch?v=CoVsMbqnNwg

----------

I worked until dawn, OpNoPro at a desk beside me, set up at his living room coffee table. And the blizzard continued to pile up snow at truly amazing rates. I suppose spending my first full winter in Canada in New Brunswick was as close to my native upbringing in Maine as you can get outside the USA. As the first dull light of day trickled in through the curtains, and our Twitter follower count topped ten thousand (in six hours), the first wave of cyber attacks on Israel cyber space began.

It started as a trickle, but around my third cup of coffee I had to turn to OpNoPro for help in simply tweeting and cataloging the attacks they were coming in that fast. Dozens of cyber attacks, launched by hackers from all over the world long frustrated that they could not strike at Israel for its injustice against the Palestinians. Clearly the Press Release, video, website and social media presence, thrown together so hastily just a few hours before - was having a profound, one could argue - geo-political, effect. The reaction from the Global Collective was brutal, and visceral. It reminded me of chub being thrown into a pool of piranha fish. As bombs rained down on Gaza, Anonymous was systematically dismantling Israel's cyberspace. It was breathtaking the speed with which *Op Israel* took hold, both in the main stream media, and within the Global Collective of Anonymous. Clearly, Anons around the world were starved to go after this particular adversary - and the veterans of the *Freedom Operations* had just given them a way. Within hours of a brave young fifteen year old Palestinian kid venturing into an IRC chat room filled with Black Hat hacktivists and asking for help, Anonymous had turned the world on its ear.

As Noon approached, an exhausted OpNopro finally went to go get some sleep. Myself, I was too stunned and excited to get more than an hour or so. Buried under a solid three feet of freshly fallen snow outside, I continued to catalog all the successful cyber attacks, and tweet them out to a voracious media. I also cataloged and tweeted the media's response to what Anonymous had done - thus creating the all important propaganda feedback loop that can fuel any protest, online or in the streets. Hundreds per hour continued to pile onto the Op Israel Twitter account. Finally after waiting what seemed like an eternity we had a newly translated and updated *Anonymous Care Package*. It was essential to the plan we cobbled together with the young Palestinian kid - whom we had conveniently turned into a media hero.

He now had his own website *VOX Palestine*, and he would be responsible for getting as many Palestinians as possible in Gaza to download this special Care Package. It was essential that as many people as possible had the software tools like the MeshNet programs if Israel made good on cutting off the Internet. Those tools, and the enclosed instructions to the Palestinians (in their own language), was how we would regain Internet contact with them should the worst happen.

The *Anonymous Care Package* also contains a wealth of other useful information, from first aid to how to make cheap but effective gas masks out of old soda bottles. While much of it had primarily been designed to support protesters in a hostile environment, and not people getting blasted with F-16's from the air - it nevertheless contained a wealth of welcome information and tools. I spent most of the evening and late into the night fielding interviews from mainstream media, who could not publish on Op Israel fast enough. After nightfall, when I could take no more and turned it over to a newly awakening OpNoPro, we had logged over ten thousand cyber attacks on Israel cyber space costing the Israeli economy an estimated one billion dollars. We had nearly twenty thousand Twitter followers, and I went to sleep contemplating the thin line between cyber activism and cyber warfare.

---------

Friday - November 16, 2012 approx. 4:00 AM ET  - "Safe House" Fredericton, New Brunswick - CANADA

I remember strange facts. And I remember clearly giving up on counting every single cyber attack at around the seventeen thousand mark. After that we have only the guestimates of the White Hats who were left to clean up our mess and comment on the wreckage we had wreaked upon Israel.

Palestinian hackers, who had unilaterally decided they were *Anonymous Palestine* - were causing mayhem from within the Gaza Strip even as bombs fell all around them. And countless Black Hats from all over the world were piling online and training their scanners on Israel cyber space. It was a free-for-all, plain and simple.

Once you've launched an Op this huge, there comes a point where all your preparations are done, all your best plans put into play - and then you just sort of ride the wave and work the media. For myself, the task of feeding a voracious mass media with interviews from "Anonymous Operation Israel" was becoming an all-consuming job. Meanwhile, just as we saw in the previous *Freedom Operations*, people began to form working groups to concentrate on particular areas of support for those being bombed in Gaza. This time around was slightly different than the so-called "Arab Spring" Freedom Ops Anonymous did, in that we were not supporting an active street revolution, but rather a besieged civilian population. One thing we used is live streaming. We assisted and promoted roof-top webcams placed there by Palestinians to live stream to the world the wanton and brutal destruction by Israel Defense Forces. A few of these live streams became quite famous, and many had very brilliant and witty rolling commentary. Working groups also monitored connectivity in Gaza, posting the status.

Meanwhile within Gaza word of Anonymous and its involvement in the conflict had spread like wildfire through the population. The hackers were fighting for them! And while this had little or no impact upon their immediate dilemma, they took huge comfort in this. For the first time in history, the Palestinians were not facing the brutality alone. Their gratitude was some of the most deep and gracious we had seen yet in these *Freedom Operations*. It first began on the live streams, the commentators going on and on about Anonymous - reporting and repeating reports on the cyber-attacks, spreading links to the *Anonymous Care Package*, and generally cheering for us and thanking us in equal measure.

But while the Palestinians cheered Anonymous on, those in other quarters were beginning to express serious concern in the western Main Stream Media. In less than 48 hours Anonymous hackers from around the world had caused hundreds of millions of dollars in damage to the Israeli cyberspace. These attacks were far from limited to only government and armed forces servers, although almost all of that category were taken offline pretty fast. The attacks had now mushroomed to include any Israel owned networks, and any nation or corporation appearing to support Israel. And the Zionist forces were begining to form up a defense. Pro-Israel hacker groups began to surface claiming they would defend against Anonymous, and even take the fight to us. But unlike some of the other pro-regime hacker groups, such as the very clever and competent *Syrian Electronic Army* or the *Iranian Cyber Army* (who famously tore us to shreds in *Behind The Mask*), the Israeli hackers simply weren't up to the challenge of either defending from, or attacking us. Even with the obvious assistance of both Mossad and the CIA, these hackers for Zionism never managed to become a factor in the unfolding conflict between Israel and Anonymous.

----------

Saturday - November 17, 2012 approx. 7:00 AM ET - "Safe House" Fredericton, New Brunswick - CANADA

The attacks on Israili cyber space had now become so intense that the traffic in and out of the entire country was begining to slow to a crawl. Just as I was sitting down with my first coffee of the day, I got a ping on PM in the IRC. It was from a screen name I had been seeing a lot of in the past few days, but had yet to meet. I flipped open the tab.

Tr1cK: Hello.

Commander X: Hi there.

Tr1cK: It's great to finally meet you. I need a favor.

Commander X: Yeah I've seen you and your Crew about, good meeting you as well. What can I do for you?

Tr1cK: I need access to the invite-only IRC channel #hack

Tr1cK had been around for about a year. He began as a regular Anon, and then formed his own Crew called Team Poison. Team Poison sometimes flew the Anonymous flag, and other times had no problem going toe to toe with us. Tr1cK was a natural leader, young, brash, and real good at hacking. In the creation of Team Poison he was beginning to show his distinctly Muslim roots, as his Crew had a serious mid-eastern feel to its online rhetoric and iconography. It didn't surprise me at all that they would take a place on the front line of this particular battle, and I had no problem plugging them into the ad hoc c&c IRC channel. I flipped open a tab, contacted the #OpIsrael channel admin and asked for an invite code. Flipping back to the PM tab with Tr1cK in it, I shot the code.

Commander X: So there you go. Anyone you trust in your Crew is welcome. I hope we can chat again soon, let me know if you need anything else.

Tr1cK: Thanks X, it's appreciated. Time to kick some Zionist ass!!

Commander X: Indeed!! Happy hunting.

Thus would begin a friendship that would last for the next three years. We'll get to why it ended later in this story.

What is important to remember now is that Tr1cK was a decent and honorable cyber warrior who ran an honest Crew, and from this day when I met him we became fast friends and close comrades in the fight.

----------

Tuesday - November 20, 2012 approx. 5:00 AM ET - "Safe House" Fredericton, New Brunswick - CANADA

It was a crystal clear, sunny, and cryogenically cold day. Not that you could see much, as the continuous snowfall for the past week had left OpNoPro's first-floor apartment essentially buried beneath meters of the white stuff. My first Canadian winter was....not starting off all that great. But thanks to my old comrade, I was at least warm and well fed, and I had a friend to sit with me as we waged cyber war on Israel.

The days were a blur of information. Taking reports of bombing runs and civilian and journalist casualties in Gaza, pushing them back out through our own propaganda channels. Setting up and pushing out rooftop live streams and other natively created media. And obviously the cyber attacks were a phenomenon unto themselves they had reached such an insane crescendo it was beyond surreal. We were now approaching fifty thousand successful cyber attacks on Israeli cyberspace, and well over a billion dollars in damage. In all the history of Hacktivism, there has never been a strike this intense or punishing against any target, much less a Nation State like Israel. And for the first time, we were hearing reports of Israeli pundits asking openly if the bombing of Gaza should not be stopped - in part because of the punishing cyber attacks and the damage they were causing to the Israel economy.

OpNoPro and I had fallen into a working pattern, combining our efforts to try and manage what had become one of the historically largest and most epic *Anonymous Operations* to date. For myself, I was beginning to wonder where this was all going. Clearly the Israelis planned on bombing Gaza for quite awhile longer, and in fact had said as much publicly. And the government was beginning to make some frightening statements vis a vis Hackers and the cyber campaign against them. Mossad was a vicious organization, and easily had enough reach to come after me here in Canada. And unfortunately my direct involvement in *Anonymous Operation Israel* was not a very well kept secret. Was Op Israel going to be one of those rare Anonymous Ops that became in essence perpetual, like Op Syria or Op Bahrain? If so, it would be a cyber battle fought in waves, with lulls of inactivity in between. So when did Operation Israel begin to....die down a little? Surely it couldn't go much longer at this intensity, or Mossad would start hunting us down one by one! All these things were on my mind when I got a ping to go to a very secret IRC back channel for an emergency meeting of the Op Israel managers.

Commander X: Yo what's up, what's the crisis?

Donatello: We have some respected Palestinian activists who want to have a few words with us. You're the last to show, so I'll give them the floor.

FreePalestine2012: I will be quick, we thank you so much for meeting with us. First, on behalf of all Palestinian people we want to thank Anonymous. No one in the world has ever stood for us before as you have, and we will never forget this.

Commander X: Thank you. Just make sure to have our backs when the shit goes down here in the West.

FreePalestine2012: We will! And now we have a favor we must ask of you. In a few hours it will be announced to the world that a cease-fire has been negotiated between Hamas and Israel. The negotiations took place in Egypt. It will be announced in 36 hours. We would like to request that Anonymous and the hackers respect the cease-fire as well.

YDT10: Well shit....

Commander X: That....has never been done before. I'm not sure we have that sort of Command & Control over such a huge Global Collective. Most of the thousands of Hacktivists involved aren't even Anons!

Donatello: We have to try, Palestinians are dying. We must give this peace a chance.

YDT10: How??

Commander X: Donatello is right, we have to try. We'll come up with a plan.

FreePalestine2012: Thank you comrades. All of Palestine thanks you. Finally, we are not alone.

Great. Now all we had to do was the impossible, put the jinn back in the bottle. Historically, all Anonymous Ops prior to this had ended one of a several ways. Either an objective was achieved, or the Op faded as it became apparent the goal would not be met, or the Op turned into a Mexican standoff like it has in Syria or Bahrain - where neither side will back down. Stopping an active Op from the top down for non-linear political reasons like this had never been done, and I would have assumed it to be impossible until today.

This was especially true of a massive historic global hacker feeding frenzy like this Op had turned into. Today, we had to make the impossible a reality, the Palestinians were counting on us. But how?

Over the next few hours we slowly devised not only a sketch of a plan, but we recruited some help. Several Crews came together and were tasked with identifying and contacting as many other allied and non-allied Crews that were engaged in *Op Israel* as they could, as quickly as they could. They were to nicely as possible request that they stand down no later than Noon ET tomorrow. The heads of the more....rational, of the Black Hat Crews were invited to a secret encrypted collaborative online "pad", a place in cyberspace where many people could work on a single document and even chat separately. That document could be saved in multiple formats by anyone with access to the pad. Over the course of the day, the following document was drafted:

Anonymous Operation Israel - Communique

Wednesday - November 21, 2012 3:00 PM ET USA

Greetings World --

For the past week, we in Anonymous have come together with many other allied cyber-activist groups from around the globe to conduct Operation Israel. Our mission was three-fold, and clearly stated: to do everything in our power to keep the innocent people of Gaza connected to the world, to interfere with the brutal aggression aimed at them by the IDF - and to help give a voice to the voiceless. We feel that we have succeeded in these goals.

We are gratified and immensely relieved, as is everyone in the world - to hear of the announced cease-fire between Hamas and the IDF.

No one in the world desires a just and lasting peace more than Anonymous. While we in the collective have no problem interfering in war, we do NOT believe it is productive to interfere with peace. We will therefore stand down immediately from all further cyber attacks upon the IDF or Israel so as not to risk this delicate and perilous cease-fire arrangement. Likewise, we encourage all those cyber groups who have joined with us to also cease and desist now from aggressive acts, and give this cease-fire a chance. We ask this NOT on behalf or for the benefit of either the government of Israel, or Hamas - but we beg it of you on behalf of the innocent people of Gaza, that they may no longer be slaughtered with impunity.

But let no one misunderstand us. Anonymous will continue to monitor the Internet and other communications lines into and out of Gaza. We will continue to watch closely BOTH sides in this war. And we will continue to advocate by all peaceful means at our disposal for a just and lasting peace for Palestine and Israel, as well as the entire world. We will be vigilant, we will be active. Operation Israel is NOT going anywhere, and the innocent people of Gaza will never be alone again. Let this Operation be an object lesson to any government or entity anywhere who believes they can turn off the Internet...

We Are Anonymous

We Are Legion

We Do Not Forgive

We Do Not Forget

EXPECT US

Web Site - www.OperationIsrael.tk

Anonymous Global - www.AnonymousGlobal.org

Op Israel Communique - http://bit.ly/Qv9yBC

----------

I maintained a closely held list of the E-Mail addresses of many hundreds of journalists from around the world. The list actually began as a gift from Barrett Brown when he departed as Spokesperson for Anonymous. By dinner the above rather....historic, Anonymous release - was in the E-Mail inboxes of hundreds and hundreds of journalists and reporters all around the globe. The media began publishing on it immediately, and I mean almost instantly. Before the list had been completely sent the first articles based on the PR were appearing in my RSS feed. As midnight approached, dozens of media outlets had already reported at length on the Press Release, and the corresponding video we had quickly produced using the PR as a script.

My Crew and the other Crews who were working on nailing down the cease-fire Crew by Crew, hacker by hacker - had reported back. It seemed that all those who were powerful enough to matter had agreed to adhere to the cease fire and quit by Noon tomorrow. Some few had even enthusiastically offered to act as enforcers and literally shut down anyone who refused to obey the cease-fire. We said gee thanks, but - ermmmm....we got this. Unbelievably, it looked like our audacious plan was actually going to work.

----------------

Tuesday - November 21, 2012 approx. 2:00 AM ET  - "Safe House" Fredericton, New Brunswick - CANADA

It's not often that an Anonymous Operation ends this way, definitively and successfully. Operation Egypt comes to mind, the celebration both in Tahir Square and in Hackerdom was a day long. But somehow this Op seemed to fit the bill, so even though we had been working hard since dawn and it was passed midnight, OpNoPro and I decided to cook steaks, drink wine, and get stoned. It was in the afterglow of that delicious meal, kicking back and enjoying the victory - when it happened. And this was hands down the best moment of *Anonymous Operation Israel*, and indeed one of my coolest memories in Anonymous, period.

The various multitude of Crews were well aware that they had about ten hours left to hack Israel cyber space, and were taking advantage of this to get some last licks in. And then it happened, in the blink of an eye. A hacker Crew hijacked the Twitter account of the *Vice Prime Minister of Israel*. Within moments the AVI and background pictures were changed, and the account began tweeting gruesome pictures of civilian casualties interspersed with pro-Palestinian and pro-Hamas propaganda. And from a propaganda stand point, especially at this stage of the cyber conflict - it was essentially a coup de grace against Israel. The utter embarassment of the double blow of the damage done finacially and the propaganda coup of Anonymous seeming at least to have dominated both cyber space and information space, was the final kick in the teeth to Israel. No one would ever forget this Operation. But the real kicker was Twitter tech support. I remember telling OpNoPro no way the account would remain in the hackers hands for more than a few minutes. They kept tweeting on it until dawn, long after dozens of media reports about them taking it had already been published.

As Noon approached, both OpNoPro and I having taken a quick cat nap behind our computers, I was sweating - literally. Would the cyber cease fire hold? The whole way it had ended last night, there was a lot of blood in the water of cyber space - would the piranhas stop feeding? I found myself wishing I believed in a god so I could pray to it now. By 1:00 PM we knew we had done it. The media agreed and they were reporting on not only the Hamas/IDF cease fire, but mentioning the fact that Anonymous had also stood down. Somehow we had achieved the impossible. We had brought Israel to its knees in cyber space, and helped to stop a war. Approximately seventy-five thousand successful cyber attacks and over two billion dollars in damage in a week. And we had managed not to lose control of the largest and most destructive hacker army ever assembled in the history of the Internet. We will never know how many more days or weeks of bombing Israel had planned for the already devastated Gaza, but it's safe to say they were actually just getting warmed up. But the fact is that even if all Anonymous did was shave one hour, or one day, off the planned operation by the IDF - then we saved countless Palestinian lives in a very direct way that was wholly new in the history of the *Anonymous Global Collective*. The gratitude of the Palestinians, which continues to this day - is something that will always bring tears to my eyes for as long as I live. It was the most cathartic moment for me as an Information Activist to see real proof that information could really and truly trump kinetic force. My ideas on what Anonymous might one day achieve went up several notches after *Anonymous Operation Israel*. But Anonymous had also aquired a whole new set of enemies and attack vectors. They were added to an already lengthy list of very powerful foes who wanted us caged, or worse. In the wake of Anonymous Operation Israel, President Obama famously declared the right to launch drone attacks against hackers. A promise he would later keep, and against one of the *actual* participants in Op Israel. The stakes in the Great Cyber War had just been raised considerably higher for Anonymous.

# THREE

## Operation Vatican

----------------------

*"For everyone who does wicked things hates
the light and does not come to the light, lest his
works should be exposed."*

~~ John 3:20

Wednesday - December 5, 2012 approx. 4:15 AM ET  - "Safe House"
Fredericton, New Brunswick - CANADA

Of all the Heads of State in the world, the Pope is probably the loneliest throne of power. Not only are you the spiritual head of an anachronistic celibate male only and dying religion, but the absolute monarch of a kingdom smaller than most pro golf courses. In that insane world of hyper-isolation and power, the Pope's butler has always held a special place. Being one of a handful of individuals who can enter and leave the Papal presence with impunity, and holding the highest security clearances possible - almost all the Pope's butlers were deeply honored and highly titled. But more than that, almost all of them ended up becoming the Pope's closest confidante and in many cases the closest thing to a best friend a man in that position can have.

This is why it came as a double shock to the world when on May 25, 2012 Pope Benedict's butler Paolo Gabriele was arrested for the largest leak of classified and secret Vatican documents in the history of Christianity. When he was arrested he had yet more stolen documents on his person. He became the first person in a very long time to actually be housed in the Vatican jail, a single cell normally used by the Swiss Guard for storage. The documents that Paolo Gabriele was charged with taking were removed directly from the Pope's office and living quarters, photocopied within the palace - and then leaked to Italian media. These documents showed how contracts were awarded to favored companies and individuals and also highlight allegations of internal power struggles with the Vatican's bank known as the Institute for Religious Works. Paolo Gabriele faced 30 years imprisoned in a single cell in a country so tiny he would be the only prisoner, making his internment essentially solitary confinement - a gross violation of his international human rights.

On October 6, 2012 Paolo Gabriele was found to be guilty of theft of secret documents, and was sentenced to 18 months and ordered to pay legal trial and investigation expenses. The ancient jail cell he was originally housed in was traded out for a more modern one built specifically to house Gabriele. Since there are no other prisoners within Vatican City State this meant that Paolo Gabriele would for all intents and purposes serve his entire sentence in solitary confinement in direct violation of his rights under the UN Human Rights Accord. But make no mistake, Paolo Gabriele was no criminal. He was a whistleblower and a hero cut from the same cloth as Edward Snowden or Chelsea Manning. His disclosure as huge for the Vatican as Snowden's or Manning's were for the USA. And not only did this man betray his "country", but he defied his faith, his God, and His Vicar on Earth. Even more than that, the Pope was his charge and his friend.

And despite months of me and my Crew lobbying everyone from WikiLeaks to the main stream media to stand up and defend this hero, no one wanted anything to do with him. And as Christmas approached and I thought about this poor man spending the holidays locked alone in a room in the Swiss Guard basement, I couldn't take it any longer. And so in the wake of Op Israel, my Crew and I launched Anonymous Operation Vatican. We prepared the usual website, and wrote up and blasted a Press release and accompanying video.

Anonymous Press Release: Operation Vatican

Wednesday - December 5, 2012

Greetings World --

The Peoples Liberation Front and Anonymous are joining forces yet again to defend whistle-blowers and fight for transparency in government. This time in the most unlikely of places, the Vatican City State.

This spring, a book was published which detailed massive corruption and wrong-doing in the highest levels of the Pope's administration. It was entitled "His Holiness" by Gianluigi Nuzzi. The book relied heavily on a massive cache of documents apparently leaked directly from the Pope's apartment/office at the Holy See.

In May of this year, Paolo Gabriele the Pope's butler was arrested for photocopying the massive trove of documents and delivering them to Nuzzi for use in his book. Today, Mr. Gabriele was convicted by the Vatican courts and sentenced to 18 months in an Italian prison (the Vatican does not have one) for this alleged disclosure of sensitive and secret material. The fact that Paolo Gabriele was almost certainly aided by someone high up in the Vatican government, most likely a Cardinal -- was never investigated by the Vatican police. Instead, Mr. Gabriele was given a very quick "trial" in a Vatican City courtroom and summarily sentenced to a year and a half in prison. The computer technician Claudio Sciarpelletti has been convicted of assisting in the disclosure and has been sentenced to two months.

Anonymous and the Peoples Liberation Front will not stand by while whistle-blowers who expose corruption in governments or corporations are persecuted and imprisoned. Whether it be Bradley Manning in the USA or Paolo Gabriele in the Vatican City State, risking everything to bring transparency to the world is an act of extreme heroism -- and deserves to be defended at all costs. The Pope is an absolute monarch, and as such has the ability to instantly pardon Paolo Gabriele and Claudio Sciarpelletti. We DEMAND that the Pope do so AT ONCE.

Until this one simple demand is met, Anonymous and the PLF will wage a relentless campaign. We will also work closely with Anonymous Italy to organize ground protests in St. Peter's Square, especially during outdoor Papal "audiences".

The Roman Catholic Church should have nothing to hide, and nothing to fear from transparency. FREE Paolo Gabriele NOW!

We Are Anonymous.

We Are Everywhere.

We Are Legion.

We Do Not Forgive.

We Do Not Forget.

Your Holiness Benedict XVI, it is too late to EXPECT US!

-------------------------------------------------------------------------

Anonymous Operation Vatican website: www.OperationVatican.tk

Peoples Liberation Front: http://www.LegionSecurity.cf

Anonymous Global: http://www.AnonymousGlobal.org

-----------

Our goal was not only to gain a pardon for Paolo Gabriele as stated in the Press Release, but to launch such a brutal strike on Vatican cyberspace that the Pope would be forced to relent and meet our demands before Christmas so he could be home with his family for the holidays. But one problem confronted us immediately.

The Pope and the Vatican appeared to have some sort of magic aura which protected them from public criticism. *Anonymous Operation Vatican* was turning out to be the exact opposite of Op Israel. It was an audience and supporter free Op! No one, not even the main stream media - wanted anything to do with Anonymous Operation Vatican. I suppose it was the religion factor that had everyone, even our fellow Anons and Hacktivists, too spooked to join the fight.

But my Crew and I were prepared to take what little help was eventually offered (most of which came eventually in the form of Mid-Eastern Anons and Hacker Crews), and do the job ourselves. After all, the Vatican cyberspace was very tiny and extremely poorly defended - why would we need more than a half dozen hackers to remove it all from the Internet? And we set to work doing just that. With OpNoPro at my side, and my Crew primed and ready - we began the strike on the cyber-domain of Vatican City State. We began with an E-Mail Bomb and Black Fax attack.

An E-Mail Bomb is a crowd-sourced strike. Essentially the goal is to enlist help on the Internet to send as many messages as possible to every single Vatican E-Mail address (which had already been harvested, along with the Vatican fax numbers). Participants would be provided with a kit containing everything from the hundreds of E-Mail addresses to suggested text and images to attach to eat up more bandwidth. E-Mail Bombs were generally dropped when it was night time for the target organization, to maximize the damage. This way you could flood the inboxes and servers while everyone slept, peacefully oblivious to the violence being done to their servers. E-Mail Bombs made a huge mess for any organization successfully targeted, and the clean-up could leave the system down for days and even weeks.

Black Fax was a similar attack in that it was crowd sourced flooding.

We would provide a kit via social media and on our websites that contained everything from web URLs where you could send international faxes for free, to suggested fax documents to send, and of course, every fax number in the Vatican. The name for this form of strike came from the old days when fax machines were like printers which sat there and printed out whatever was sent to them. Those days are passed, and even in a world as archaic as that of the Vatican, they had long since moved to mostly electronic fax inboxes similar to E-Mail. So the times of simply sending black pieces of paper (from which the attack got its name) in a Black Fax campaign in order to run out the ink and paper were gone, and we could send pictures, memes, and our manifesto instead.

-----------

Thursday - December 6, 2012 approx. 6:00 AM ET  - "Safe House" Fredericton, New Brunswick - CANADA

This morning the takedown of the Vatican network began in earnest. As the Italian and Vatican media (nearly the only MSM to have reported on Op Vatican) began to take notice that something was afoot from the consternation of the Vatican security and IT people, my own Crew and other hacktivists were slowly infiltrating the Vatican network, laying back doors, exfiltrating data, and setting the stage for probably the most dramatic cyber attack the Vatican has ever seen. OpNoPro manned the IRC and tried to keep order in the small but lively *Op Vatican* channels. I fielded media interview requests and networked and interfaced with the various hackers, cells, and crews working the Operation. I also worked with my own Crew to target our own chosen front in this battle, the Swiss Guard. But our scans had left me with the conclusion that they were so insecure and unmanned that it was more a question of which way we wanted to fuck them up first, rather than *if* we could mess with them.

**49**

I decided to task my Crew with further exploits into the Swiss Guard network while I distracted the defenders with a solo attack. The scans had shown that among the numerous vulnerabilities within the Swiss Guard network, some were almost laughable in their simplicity. The network was served from old unpatched apache boxes within the Swiss Guard compound that were *Slowloris* susceptible. With a single *Slowloris Canon* fired from my laptop in New Brunswick, I was able to turn all of the public-facing aspects of the Swiss Guard's network into a smoking crater in cyber space in about ten minutes. It took them several days to recover from that attack alone, but it was just a smoke screen. Under cover of my fire, lasting approximately twenty-four hours, elements from Africa and the Mid-East infiltrated the databases of the Swiss Guard. Over the coming days they would use that access to pulverize the Swiss Guard with punishing waves of E-Mail dumps, followed in step and beat by defacements of their public facing pages.

-----------

Friday - December 7, 2012 approx. 7:00 AM ET  - "Safe House" Fredericton, New Brunswick - CANADA

The decimation of the Vatican network had begun to spread beyond the central government targets. Obscure Saint's websites being hosted in nunneries on Windows XP boxes were being owned at a hysterical rate. Archbishops and Cardinals lost their web presence to laughing and jeering hackers wearing Guy Fawkes Masks. Nothing was sacred, and nothing was safe if it ended with the .va domain name. This morning we received an encrypted message from a Vatican insider who wanted us to know what was happening at the highest levels in the Papal Palace:

"You guys have no idea the effect you have had. The entire upper echelon of the Curia are in a complete panic over the rolling cyber attacks. They are actually afraid (because someone told them to be so) that you might turn off the electricity in the Vatican. Keep up the great work, a few here are laughing at them and with you. Our man will be free soon.

P. S. When the Holy Father was briefed on you, they told him you were called Anonymous and your motto was 'We Are Legion. We Do Not Forgive. We Do Not Forget. Expect Us', he turned very pale. When they showed him a picture of the mask, we thought he would faint, and he ended the meeting unexpectedly. The whole biblical connotation thing, you know. He was really rattled and they even called his physician."

Not many people begin their day by opening up an E-Mail like that. If our source was to be believed, we had terrified the Vatican, and even the Pope himself. Good. I investigated this "source" as best I could, consulted my team, and using some small validating evidence the source had sent, we judged him/her to be legitimate. We began to wage a relentless and separately manned information campaign designed to play to the prelates worst fears about "Legion" who had become the "demons in their wires". Across social media, in particular on Twitter and Facebook, we began a merciless campaign of memes, re-tweeting the worst of the child sex scandals, banking corruption, basically anything we could, all branded up with the "Legion" Mask and our darkest iconography that the Pope had actually been shown a picture of - so we had been told by our "source". If the old white men who ran their little religious kingdom, who feared transparency so much they would imprison one of their own in a broom closet, were that afraid of us, we would make them yet more afraid. The oldest propaganda machine on earth was about to have its first run in with the Internet, and be handed its ass in an epic faceplant.

In many ways we began to fall into a very similar pattern as the just concluded *Anonymous Operation Israel*, with the obvious exception of scale. Both our target surface as well as our participation was minuscule compared to Op Israel. Which actually came as a welcome relief to be honest. It is much easier to control the message and attack vectors to achieve precise results in a smaller Op. We definitely had our own little, admittedly audience free, smashy smashy party going on against the Vatican. And strangely, the sort of emotional motive seemed to be very similar to Op Israel, pent up aggravation at an ancient and seemingly implacable evil that was finally being laid low, however symbolically - and served just a little justice in the process. It was a fun Op. But I began to wonder from all the rumors and leaks if the poor old Pope would survive the chaos being inflicted on a part of his kingdom he couldn't even understand.

-----------

Wednesday - December 12, 2012 approx. 5:30 AM ET - "Safe House" Fredericton, New Brunswick - CANADA

Today we were going to deploy what was at the time a relatively new information weapon, but which has since become a standard hacktivist tool; namely a "Twitter Storm". Originally there was even an Anonymous created software to help people participate in a Twitter Storm. I'm not sure why such an automated approach has fallen out of favor, or if Twitter simply made it more difficult to utilize their API for such "malicious" purposes. A Twitter Storm is a crowdsourced action designed to create a huge wave of attention rolling across social media, namely Twitter and secondary, Facebook. Its principal purpose is to either cause a particular set of hashtags to trend, usually globally, on Twitter, or to hijack someone else's trending hashtag such as say #Superbowl - and ride their wave for effect.

Sometimes both of these principal effects are engaged in truly massive worldwide Twitter Storms that can make the news cycle for days. It was and remains an extremely effective tool if applied properly.

To run a Twitter Storm you put together a "kit", usually in a place like PasteBin. The kit contains instructions and goals for the Storm, suggested Tweets to copy/paste during the Storm, and tips for being the most effective. The start time and duration of the Twitter Storm will then be disseminated along with this starter kit via social media. Retweets don't work, all tweets must be unique to count towards the trend. Thus the idea of automation. But many people who can only participate part time in *Anonymous Operations* love to help with these sorts of crowd-sourced strikes. If the timing and preparation is right, they can make a huge impact.

Today we had just the right moment, that history had just handed our little Op. Because today, for the first time in history, the Pope was going to get a Twitter account!  And we knew from the press release that he was going to send his first Tweet in person, so a concurrent Twitter Storm using both the #FreePaoloGabriele as well as hijacking the hashtags the Vatican had suggested, could actually result in the Pope seeing the Storm and having it explained to him what we were doing to his little publicly broadcast social media ceremony. Luckily the Internet had seen the lulz in disrupting the Popes well choreographed entrance into social media, and the pre-Storm hype indicated many thousands of activists were raring to go with witty Tweets, and not a few humorous (and sometimes tasteless) memes. The Twitter Storm against the Pope was a resounding success, and the disruption of this little media event remains a pivotal moment in the effort to free Paolo Gabriele.

-----------

Friday - December 21, 2012 approx. 11:30 AM ET  - "Safe House"
Fredericton, New Brunswick - CANADA

Our goal was to free Paolo Gabriele from his Swiss Guard basement
room "prison" before Christmas so he could be home with his family
for the Holidays. I will admit that until early this morning, I was
beginning to despair that our strike on the Vatican would fail, at least
in our deadline we set in our demands. All that changed to elation
among my Crew this morning when our "source" within the Vatican
dropped one last leak on us. One short sentence:

"He will be freed later today, and pardoned by Papal Decree."

And now we awaited the fateful announcement from the Vatican Press
Office. It came late in the morning. By lunchtime we were getting
drunk and watching live television video of Paolo Gabriele  being led
out of his Swiss Guard "prison" cell and greeted by his adoring
family. He gave a brief statement, and he was unapologetic for the
leak, which had shown massive scandal at the Vatican going back
decades. And *Anonymous* had just knocked up another victory against
a powerful global foe. And in the process made yet another very
powerful enemy, one that had its own legacy of "never forgetting"
going back two millennia.

   While Operation Vatican was a bit personal for me, in that it never
really gained traction among my fellow western Information Activists,
I still feel very strongly it was absolutely the right thing to do. If we
are going to stand vehemently and militantly for whistleblowers who
leak material on governments and corporations, we must afford the
same defense to those who bring transparency to the world's religions
- and especially one that is unique like the Vatican in that it is also a
legal Nation State. I will never see Paolo Gabriele as anything less
than equally as heroic as Chelsea Manning or Edward Snowden.

And for him, he didn't just betray his government, but his Faith, his Pope, boss, and friend, and quite possibly his God. It took huge amazing courage, and his lack of defense while we Information Activists so openly fought for Manning was simply unacceptable to me.

Not long after *Anonymous Operation Vatican* bent a Pope to its will and freed a whistleblower, Pope Benedict resigned the Papacy, something that has only happened one other time in the two thousand year history of the Catholic Church. He left the Papacy looking positively haggard and haunted - nearly dead actually. I would love to think that in some small way *Anonymous Operation Vatican* helped to hasten this wicked old man from the *Throne of St. Peter.*

# FOUR

## *Operation Roll RedRoll*

**-------------------**

*"This disclosure is about the truth. This disclosure is about setting examples. If you lie, if you are corrupt, if you commit wrong doing - you will be found out. It will be revealed, and justice will be served."*

~~ LocalLeaks

• • •

Sunday - December 23, 2012 approx. 11:00 AM ET - "Safe House" Fredericton, New Brunswick - CANADA

On August 22, 2012 two members of the Big Red High School football team in Steubenville, Ohio - USA were arrested and charged with the rape and kidnapping of an out of town 16 year old girl that took place on August 11th. At the time of this gang rape, the girl was intoxicated and unconscious. The victim had been intentionally drugged with a "date rape" intoxicant. She was photographed and video was taken of her in this condition, and there is evidence that she was hauled in a comatose state to multiple parties - and almost certainly raped by more members of the local high school football and wrestling team than just the two players who currently stand charged. There is even evidence that she was urinated upon during this hideous assault. Despite all this, it looked as though a town rife with corruption, cronyism, illegal gambling and fixated upon their star high school football team (a major economic revenue engine) were prepared to orchestrate a major cover-up in order to sweep the entire affair under the rug. As this chapter will document, this cover-up was perpetrated by people in the high school administration, local government and law enforcement.

A cell within Anonymous called *Knight Security* took up the cause of giving a voice to the victim of this horrible crime, and began unraveling this conspiracy of silence designed to protect a group of these high school football players who had become well known to their fellow students as "The Rape Crew". Fueled by intelligence they had received from many students at Big Red High School, they launched *Anonymous Operation Roll RedRoll* by releasing a press release and video. Take careful note of the various screen capture images of pictures taken by these monsters of this poor defenseless girl, and note their many comments made in tweets and Facebook posts regarding their crime (now since deleted).

The Op was immediately and heatedly controversial within Anonymous USA, and by late morning this individual and his Crew Knight Security were taking heat from some fairly heavy hitting and influential Anons. The founder and leader of *Knight Security* was a hacktivist called KYAnonymous.

KYanon and I had bumped into each other here and there in Annymous circles, and I was impressed with his zeal. He and his Crew had taken a special liking to going up against rape culture in the USA, and so it didn't surprise me when the uproar began and I found him and his Crew neck deep in the middle of the mess. And the mess already had a name, *Anonymous Operation Roll RedRoll*. OpNoPro and I watched with mild amusement as KYanonymous got knocked about in the twitter Time Lines for starting an Op not everyone agreed with. As I said some fairly influential Anons were nay sayers apparently. Finally I told OpNoPro I was thinking of intervening on KYanon's behalf, and he concurred. We both liked the cause of standing up for this poor girl and maybe bringing this rape gang to justice. And neither of us had anything but positive interactions with either KYanonymous or his Crew Knight Sec. I flipped open a Twitter DM tab and pinged him.

@CommanderXanon: Hey, what's up? I was wondering if maybe you'd like a hand. Me and my Crew like your Op, and I'm willing to stand up publicly and get your back if you want.

@KYAnonymous: Wow, honored X. I'll take any help I can get at this point. You're a legend man, if you stand up many will listen to you.

@CommanderXanon: Well, I don't know about the legend part. And I have my own fairly dedicated cadre of haters, that might actually be a downside for you to consider.

But sure, me and my Crew are in. Consider us a part of the Op. But it's your Op KY, I'm not running this. You started it and you finish it, understood?

@KYAnonymous: Got it, and thanks. Any immediate suggestions?

@CommanderXanon: Yes. The rally today was weak. Get Occupy Steubenville involved, I researched them and for a small town it's a decently organized Occupy. And make sure to bring a bullhorn, a sound system, and batteries for both next time. Line up speakers in advance via social media. Finally, check out a little something I am involved in called "LocalLeaks" at www.LocalLeaks.ml I think that will be helpful tool for you moving forward. Begin making your Crew and the world aware of the site on social media. Let's see if we can't at least get enough info leaked that we can get a rough outline of how this coverup was engineered.

@KYAnonymous: Making notes now X, we'll do it. I can't thank you enough for this, it means a lot.

@CommanderXanon: Let's just stay focused on what success is here, let's find out what happened to this girl and who did it. Then get them in front of a jury.

@KYAnonymous: I have a feeling we'll have the information we need shortly.

@CommanderXanon: Indeed. Well that sure will make things interesting. Let me ask you, any word from the girl or her family since you let drop the Press Release and video for the Op?

@KYAnonymous: Strictly between you and me? Yes.

They are happy for the help, these boys are ready to straight up skate for what they did to their daughter. The small town system is rigged around industrial grade high school football.

@CommanderXanon: Ok then, try and get it a little tighter for tomorrow. I'll send out your PR and video to the Anonymous Media List. Let's both push the idea of LocalLeaks and see if we can get someone to dump some goodies on us.

-----------

Wednesday - December 26, 2012 approx. 7:30 AM ET  - "Safe House" Fredericton, New Brunswick - CANADA

The daily protests, in driving snowstorms no less - were growing constantly. What started as dozens huddled together on the Steubenville Courthouse steps had now become several hundred, and tomorrow's protest held the possibility of a couple of thousand. That was a lot for a small town of only fifty thousand or so. As I suggested, KYAnonymous had brought in Occupy Steubenville to help with the organization on the ground so that he and his Crew *Knight Security* could concentrate more on the cyber aspects of what we wanted to achieve.

I am actually the Editor In Chief of LocalLeaks, This morning when I opened up the submissions box at LocalLeaks, I found we had a submission! A leak! At the begining of *Anonymous Operation Roll RedRoll* the lead Crew *Knight Security* had hacked a Steubenville High football fan website and its servers because it was rumored that its owner was deeply involved in the corruption surrounding this lucrative high school football franchise.

Initially there had been a deface of the front page, but apparently files were also taken because once I unpacked the leak from the submissions box I found the entire E-Mail spool of the website owner. So I spent the day building the now infamous "The Steubenville Files" at LocalLeaks, and blasting a PR announcing the new section and the inaugural leak. Within hours, the main stream media had made the Steubenville Files a viral sensation - and the floodgates opened up.

The leaks began trickling in just after Noon, and by evening we were receiving several dozen an *hour*. This level of leaks into the LocalLeaks submission box would continue for weeks. I could litterally just keep hitting the refresh button and there were new submissions. Clearly this was a city dying to liberate itself from serious endemic corruption, and we had given them the only viable opportunity to come along so far. But something was happening that went beyond Steubenville. LocalLeaks had had a few minor disclosures, but the platform had struggled to find support and an audience. Not only was all that clearly changing, but we were now making disclosure history, for surely no disclosure platform, not even WikiLeaks, had ever received this many discrete leaks from individual sources in such a short space of time.

As evening approached I turned to OpNoPro for advice. We had printed out the most tantalizing and informative of the leaks, we had piles of them laying all over the table and desk. The sources were all over the place, from local law enforcment to people living in the Sheriff's own houshold. And clearly there was a pattern here, but how to see it? How could we string all this disparate data into a coherent theory that would prove a cover-up in Steubenville? I searched for data analysis software and there were some programs that might be helpful, but they cost a fortune. But when I saw the screen shots it gave me an idea. Grabbing a twenty off OpNoPro I hit the store and bought colored string, tacks, and scissors.

Returning to the apartment, I proceeded to walk around OpNoPro's living room, tacking leaks to the wall in what at first appeared to be a random pattern. But when I started thoughtfully applying different colored string, OpNoPro, who was watching my work intently, began to nod in understanding.

I had not chosen the string colors randomly. Green was for money, red for violence, purple for gambling or drugs. I worked for hours, long into the night. Leaks continued to pour in and OpNoPro would print and sort them for me. By dawn we could begin to see the outline of how a young girl could be gang raped by six boys in front of dozens of witnesses (even taking pictures and sharing them on their mobile devices) and not be charged with anything. I spent the next week puzzling over OpNoPro's living room walls, printing and adding new leaks to the collage, and then updating the Steubenville Files on the LocalLeaks website as we gained new insights into what really hapened to Jane Doe, who did it, and who was protecting them.

-----------

Thursday - January 3, 2013 approx. 7:30 AM ET  - "Safe House" Fredericton, New Brunswick - CANADA

I was going through the submission box, trying to see if anything earth shattering had been leaked during the night regarding Steubenville. The third one I opened made me spill my coffee all over OpNoPro's carpet. It was the single biggest leak ever for LocalLeaks, I knew this within ten seconds. And even then as I watched the video a second time unable to believe we had this, I knew it was a game changer not only for the Op, but for my disclosure platform as well.

It was a video. Clearly one of the boys we had identified as a member of the infamous Steubenville "Rape Crew" had his phone, or more likely the cloud storage attached to it, hacked.

The entire nauseating video was of one Michael Colin Nodianos a Steubenville High student who we had identified as not only a member of the "Rape Crew", but one of the actual attackers. The video was shot in the basement of one of the boys, *while the attack on Jane Doe was still ongoing*. It shows Nodianos in a basement (with a rifle nearby) as he brags about being one of the rapists, and described how Jane Doe is actually still there, naked outside on the lawn, and how they had just peed on her. The video goes on for a long time, and is so difficult to watch that we released it with a viewer warning attached.

After watching it twice I showed it to OpNoPro. We both realized that we were about to sieze the western news cycle, and turn Steubenville, already a hot bed, inside out. This was going to change everything. As I rushed to cook us both a good breakfast and brewed a gallon of coffee, myself and OpNoPro discussed how best to proceed with this disclosure. As we feasted and talked, we planned out the release for the Noon news cycle. That didn't leave much time for details like the press release, but this video wasn't going to need a lot of supporting material in order to have an impact. The impact would be immediate, and devastating.

-----------

Saturday - January 7, 2013 approx. 8:00 AM ET  - "Safe House" Fredericton, New Brunswick - CANADA

This morning found me working frantically with the production crew of Democracy Now! hosted by the epic Amy Goodman. This would be my second appearance on DN! and I was just as nervous as the first time. Amy Goodman was not only a pre-eminent and award winning journalist, but she was an icon and one of the founders and innovators of the independent media movement which many people in information activism simply take for granted today.

The technical requirements for me to safely do television given my situation are daunting to say the least. It's why I do so few of these sorts of interviews. Finally, we got it right and I was able to send a stable and encrypted video signal to the studio of Democracy Now!

I was then summarily banished to the virtual "green room" to listen to the other guests and await my turn to be on the show. After some time passed, Amy rolled with my intro and I flipped the switch on my mic to talk to the world about *Anonymous Operation Roll RedRoll*.

AMY GOODMAN: I want to turn to the hacktivist from Anonymous, to "X," a pseudonym for security reasons. Can you tell us what it is that you did, that your group did?

"X": Hi, Amy. Thanks for having me on today. I think, to begin with, it's important to understand that this action involved three separate entities that are overlapping and coordinated, but separate. The cyber-action, which involved the hacking and the various other cyber-aspects, were conducted by Anonymous in a very specific cell within Anonymous known as KnightSec. And then the ground protests, which were - took place on two Saturdays in a row—this last Saturday and the one before - were handled by Occupy Steubenville, so that was their responsibility. And then the third sort of part of the puzzle was the Local Leaks, which is the disclosure platform that we have, which released a great - just a copious amount of information on this case. And so, it's important to understand that those three elements were involved.

AMY GOODMAN: I just want to say, especially for radio listeners who cannot see, that you're wearing a Guy Fawkes mask, and your head is covered. Your voice is masked, as well as your name. Why are you doing this anonymously?

"X": For security purposes. Actually, I've been on your show before.

The last time I was on the air, I was still anonymous with a small "a," and I was apprehended shortly after I appeared on your show last time by the FBI. And for a number of reasons, because I felt that the prosecution was political against myself, I chose to flee into exile, and I'm in Canada now. And so, my name is actually known to most people.

You could research me and easily find out who I am. My appearance is masked because I've altered by appearance since I've gone into exile. And I'm now a fugitive, so I've altered my appearance. But I keep the name "X" because, to be honest with you, I kind of like it.

AMY GOODMAN: How did you get a hold—explain the video that your group, that Anonymous, that you got a hold of, that you released, what this 12-minute video showed.

"X": Well, I think it's apparent to anybody who can stomach watching it for the entire 12 minutes. I, myself, here at our location - we've been working night and day on this operation, and I've watched it at least a dozen times, and it makes me sick each time we watch it. I think it speaks for itself. These young men were sitting around immediately after the crime took place - that's clear from what they say in the video. One person even gets up at one point and leaves in disgust and goes to check on the victim to see if the victim is OK. So the victim is still nearby, still - the crime is still in progress, in essence, when this video was shot. And a number of people are implicated in the video, including the subject of the video; Michael Nodianos implicates himself in this crime. So I think the video speaks for itself. And, you know, I can't imagine how the police do not see this as further evidence and do not levy charges against the people in the video.

AMY GOODMAN: What are you, Monika, calling for right now? Right now, two young people have been charged. There is a lot of community support for the football players. Wasn't there reference in the video to Duke and the lacrosse players?

MONIKA JOHNSON HOSTLER: There was. And very much so, like "X" said, I had to actually watch the 12-minute video in increments, because it was sickening to my stomach to hear men, especially of this age, talk about how dead she was. And one of them, I think, even alluded to, if this was your daughter or your wife in 10 years, you wouldn't be saying this, and he said, "Yes, I would."

So, for me, especially as a parent, not just as an advocate, it is sickening to hear the degree of which they go on and carry on about how much she was raped. And so, the correlation to Duke was, she was raped more than the Duke lacrosse players raped.

AMY GOODMAN: And so, what do you -

MONIKA JOHNSON HOSTLER: And so, what we are calling - what we are calling for is not just how this is handled in Steubenville, Ohio, but really asking America to take a hard look at ourselves in how we are - handle sexual violence and rape in our country. I think we've been able to point our fingers and turn our heads to rapes that have happened in other countries and not held ourselves accountable as Americans to say that we absolutely still have a culture of rape, where women and girls are still degraded and dehumanized, and rape is in the fabric of this country. And unfortunately, I would think, centuries later, that we would be further along in terms of our response, but yet we still see Americans blaming victims. So, in terms of our overall response, we're calling for America to take a hard look at itself and really think about the culture that we're raising our kids in and the things that we are allowing to happen by not acknowledging, as a community, as a society, the importance of supporting the rape victim.

And I do want to go back briefly to something you asked Kristie earlier about the rape victim recalling her story or what happened. And what I'd like to point out to your listeners and viewers is, oftentimes rape victims don't consider what happened to them rape.

Just as Kristie described, in this case, she was intoxicated, inebriated, that she wasn't able to actually recall what happened, which is often the case that we hear with drug-facilitated or alcohol-facilitated rapes. So I think it's important for people to understand, before we begin to blame the victim, when a victim recalls their story in pieces, it is often because of cases like this where it's difficult to recall the incidents that happen, especially when they're intoxicated or inebriated.

AMY GOODMAN: Kristen, can you talk about the role of social media in exposing the story - first Alexandria, the blogger, then Anonymous?

KRISTEN GWYNNE: Social media has played an interesting role in the story from the beginning, because without it, just prosecuting the case at all would have been difficult because so much of the evidence was tweets and Facebook posts and videos that kids put up on YouTube. And what Alexandria Goddard did was take screen shots of everything before the kids were smart enough, I guess, to realize that they needed to delete them. So she was able to compile evidence that....

AMY GOODMAN: And who is she?

KRISTEN GWYNNE: She was a blogger, a local - for the website Prinniefied.com, and she was also from the town. So she had, I guess, a personal interest in investigating further, because she said, from the minute she heard about the case, she believed that the football players were being treated specially because the town has so much invested in the team. And then, once Anonymous caught hold of it, they took it even further by exposing more—more tweets and then, of course, the video, which was just a stunning, I guess, testament to the rape culture in America and in this town, in particular.

AMY GOODMAN: Finally, "X," can you talk about OpPedoChat and talk about - well, I'm looking at Wired magazine.

"It could indicate that this is the project of one subsection of Anonymous, which would explain the slightly different tone to the information release. This isn't the first anti-paedophile project from the group, either." And then it goes on to talk about the past ones.

"X": Sure, Amy, I'll be happy to, but I just want to point out one last thing on the Steubenville subject. There's more to this than just a rape that's being covered up because of football and because of legitimate revenue within that community.

We have uncovered - Anonymous has uncovered a gigantic gambling ring in Steubenville that, you know, is - probably half of the revenue in that community is underground, and it involves gambling, involves drugs. So, there's more to this than this. This story is about corruption. It's about a sick fascination and fixation with football. And so, I encourage people to go to LocalLeaks and look at the information that we've revealed, because this goes deeper than just rape.

Regarding OpPedoChat -

AMY GOODMAN: We have 10 seconds.

"X": OpPedoChat is an operation by Anonymous to uncover pedophiles on social media and to out them and to get them removed from social media and, hopefully, arrested and convicted for their crimes.

AMY GOODMAN: Well, Commander X, I want to thank you for being with us, hacktivist with the group Anonymous. Also, thank you to Monika Johnson Hostler with the National Alliance to End Sexual Violence, as well as to Kristen Gwynne.

-----------

Friday - January 11, 2013 approx. 8:00 AM ET  - "Safe House" Fredericton, New Brunswick - CANADA

By now the shitstorm swirling around Steubenville was in full swing. Nearly daily protests involving thousands of Mask wearing Anons, feminists, and just folks who supported Jane Doe, were tying up downtown Steubenville relentlessly. Everything from City Hall to the Sheriff's Department had been hacked so many times some of them just stopped trying to fix them.

Thanks to me and my Crew's intervention on behalf of KYAnonymous and *Knight Security*, *Anonymous Operation Roll RedRoll* was gaining global concensus and participation. But as the Editor In Chief of *LocalLeaks*, my faithful side-kick, OpNoPro and I had our hands full. Hundreds of seperate leaks had been submitted, with more pouring in every hour. And while OpNoPro's living room was now a mass of printed leaks and colored string, we were actually starting to see a clear picture of just exactly what was going on in Stubenville that could allow a gang rape to go unpunished.

OpNoPro and I were working on yet another daily update to the now world-famous *Steubenville Files* when our world came to a screeching halt as an annoncement began flooding our Twitter Time Lines and other social media.

Aaron Swartz was dead.

Aaron Swartz was a genius child-prodigy coder who among many things created Reddit and innovated RSS news feeds. All before he was old enough to vote. At five years old, Aaron wrote his first piece of software. And now, because of the exact same political persecution against Information Activivts by USDOJ using the outdated and brutal CFAA that drove me from my own country, had now killed our beloved Aaron. Aaron was dead by his own hand at a mere twenty-six years old. They had hounded him for years, for simply downloading too many scientific journals which he had a right to download anyway. The FBI tormented him, his family, his girl friend and even his ex-girl friend.

All simply to prove a point and strike a blow at those "free information" nut jobs. Aaron had hung himself in his apartment. And my world was unhinged.... So it wasn't enough for the USA to imprison Information Activists for decades, or to run us out of our own country. Now they were going to hound our families and us....to death.

And oh my god how they had now taken the *very* best of us. Kind, decent, caring, even patriotic Aaron was a saint. There was not a bad bone in his body. Dear.... that's how I would have described him. He was a dear and incredibly intelligent wonder boy. And they had driven him to his death. The slow building rage that had been building against the government of the USA for its war on Anonymous, WikiLeaks, and Information Activists, boiled over. It had gone from being simple political resolve and revolutionary zeal...to *hatred*. By the end of the day, and to this day - that's what Aaron's death gave me. A burning hatred of, and determination to destroy completely, the government of the USA. *Never forgive, never forget....*

-----------

Sunday - January 15, 2013 approx. 8:00 AM ET  - "Safe House" Fredericton, New Brunswick - CANADA

Today we would release through LocalLeaks the first draft of the final report on precisely what happened to Jane Doe on that fateful night, who did it to her - and how. OpNoPro and I had stayed up all night polishing and editing the final section of the now famous *Steubenville Files*. And no matter how many times I've read this report, it still breaks my heart and makes me cry.

-- What REALLY Happened That Night --

We have received an extraordinary set of particular leaks from a number of young people in Steubenville who were witness to various parts of this horrendous crime. From this material, we have been able to piece together a timeline of events on that fateful night in August 2012. During this description, we will refer to the victim as "Jane Doe".

After being convinced, with some amount of coaxing - to attend the parties that night with the "Rape Crew" by Mark Cole's girlfriend Santoro, Jane Doe was picked up at a volleyball team party she was attending in the early evening of August 11th and transported in a vehicle with Richmond, Mays and Cole in it. Jane Doe was administered a "date rape" drug snuck into her drink almost immediately, possibly while still in the vehicle en route to the night's "festivities". In any case, she has no memories after being picked up. The first party of the night was at the home of Assistant Coach Rick Cameletti, where Michael Nodianos, Charlie Keenan, Cody Saltsman, and Anthony Craig were already engaged in heavy drinking and drug use. At this location Jane Doe was raped multiple times by Richmond and Mays and at least two other assailants from the "Rape Crew". At that point the "party" went on the move. They first stopped at another Assistant Coach's home, Coach Belerdine. Both Belerdine and his sister were present at this time. Jane Doe was again sexually assaulted at this party. They hit the road again with an unconscious Jane Doe in tow. While en route to Mark Cole's house, Jane was again raped and sodomized in the back seat of a vehicle - and this was video recorded by Mark Cole who was in the front seat. Her attackers in the car were again Mays and Richmond. Once they arrived at Mark Cole's house Jane Doe was carried to the basement where she was again raped multiple times by multiple attackers, one of which was Michael Nodianos. Also at the Cole residence, Jane Doe was orally raped by Trent Mays.

**70**

Finally, having sated themselves and exhausted any further entertainment that Jane Doe could provide for these animals, she was unceremoniously dumped (still unconscious) onto the front lawn of the Cole residence - where at least one member of the "Rape Crew" proceeded to urinate on her. At some point in the early morning hours of August 12th, a still unconscious Jane Doe was transported to her home in West Virginia - where she was deposited on the front lawn of her families home. She was discovered there by her parents at dawn.

-----------

Just after the final release of the *Steubenville Files* a personal thank you note from Jane Doe was quietly circulated among a few of us who had worked so hard on *Anonymous Operation Roll RedRoll*.

Dear Anonymous --

I wanted to thank you all from the bottom of my heart. What you did for me was priceless. By standing with me, by making me not alone anymore - you gave me back my dignity.

I feel like I am an honorary member of Anonymous. I will never forget what you did for me.

ALL MY HEART -- Jane Doe

-----------

In short order, a Grand Jury was called into existence. There were indictments of students and coaches - many were caught up in the dragnet. Grand Juries have broad investigatory powers, and this one went into all the dark corners that LocalLeaks had shone a light into. Two of the young men that LocalLeaks had identified as having repeatedly violated Jane Doe were eventually convicted and sent to prison for a couple of years. A soft jeuvenile detention facility.

Things did not turn out so well for the Information Activist and hero Anon who started it all, KYAnonymous. Feeling the FBI closing in on him with their CFAA swords drawn, KYAnonymous threw down his last card. He stepped out into the stage lights and took off his Mask. And he did it, as we say in the Hacker Underground - 'like a sir'.

Due to many serious death threats and other personal security issues, he was forced to use donated funds to purchase armed security and body Guards for himself and his entourage. The event was well attended, and fairly dramatic. KYAnonymous stepped forward, pulled off his Mask - and introduced himself: "hello, my name is Deric Lostutter, and it is a relief to take off this Mask and face you".

Eventually, Deric's house was raided by the FBI - and in due course he was indicted, convicted, and sentenced to slightly more time in prison than the rapists he helped expose and bring to justice recieved. By then he was married, and his wife was expecting a child. As this book goes to print, he is still serving his sentence. To this day, I have no idea who the source of any of the leaks, big or small, that LocalLeaks recieved during *Anonymous Operation Roll RedRoll* actually were. If Deric was a source for any of them, he never admitted it to me privately, in court or publicly. But if he was, then he's even more of a hero than he was for initiating and seeing through the epic and historic *Anonymous Operation Roll RedRoll*.

It is my belief that "rape culture", which thrives everywhere from the heartland of the USA to India, is one of the greatest human rights challenges of our time.

If we are to confont something so vicious and violent, we will need to be open minded to occasional "vigilante actions" that fall outside the strict purview of the "law". When that rape culture is protected and covered up by officials in the over-riding interest of profit, both legitimate and illicit - transgressive action may well be the only way to get any justice at all for the victims of these horrible crimes. The Transparency Model of disclosure, innovated by Julian Assange and WikiLeaks, and emulated by myself with LocalLeaks, is a powerful new tool in helping to unmask culpability in such a vast network of corruption as that which we discovered in Steubenville.

In that regard, LocalLeaks not only had a huge impact in the successful *Anonymous Operation Roll RedRoll*, but we managed to make disclosure history. What we came to term the "disclosure event" in Steubenville resulted in many hundreds of separate discrete leaks pouring into our submission box in a mere 15 days. Main Stream Media caught onto this, and a couple of articles were written just focusing on the historic nature of this "disclosure event". WikiLeaks even came to our support, and Jay Liederman my attorney demanded to be recognized as the official legal counsel for LocalLeaks. Everyone from the waitress who served the Sheriff, to a member of his own family actually living in his house, were leaking everything from pictures of his SSI card to his voice mail messages. Leaks poured in from law enforcement officers, teachers, civil servants, and just regular citizens familiar with the corruption in their community. It's like the entire community saw LocalLeaks as a virtual confessional, and were using us to cleanse their city. There remains to this day much un-released and un-analyzed material leaked to us during *Anonymous Operation Roll RedRoll* in our secret archives. Perhaps when Deric is released from prison, we'll dump the rest of it on LocalLeaks.

# FIVE

## *Operation Bahrain*

---------------------

*"The tipping point for me was watching things deteriorate in Bahrain, and knowing that the situation there is highly influenced and dependent on the ability of the U.S. press to report accurately on that story."*

~~ Amber Lyon - Journalist

• • •

Friday - February 15, 2013 approx. 7:00 AM ET  - "Safe House"
Fredericton, New Brunswick - CANADA

In the tiny Gulf nation of Bahrain, led by one "King" Khalifa - the manufacture, sale, or possession of a *Guy Fawkes Mask* is a felony punishable by up to ten years in prison. This is the story of how that came to be. This is the story of how a small group of western Information Activists banded together with desperate pro-democracy protesters in the dying days of one of the world's last "absolute monarchies", and turned the Kingdom of Bahrain inside out. This is a union and struggle that persists at least until the printing of this book. And as long as there is breath in my body and a pulse in my veins, there will be an *Anonymous Operation Bahrain*. Because I will live long enough to visit a truly free Bahrain, where I will straight away visit the tomb of this "King" Khalifa, and spit on his grave.

I will plague this "monarchy" for the rest of my natural life. I have heard that there is a fatawa, a death warrant - secretly issued for me by the Bahrain "King". I say fucking bring it dictator. Because that is all "King" Khalifa is, a petty tin-pot dictator who is brutally abusing his own "subjects" in a desperate bid to keep it from not being the middle ages anymore. I will out live you, you bastard "King". I will plague you until the day your old sorry ass pops from a stroke, and I will make sure your entire fucking bloodline spends the rest of their days in exile, or preferably in prison where they belong. I will outlast and defeat you all, you fucking animals.

And I am far from alone within the *Hacker Underground* sharing this passionate hatred of this petty tyrant. Operation Bahrain remains to this day very active and very well supported by the Global Collective. In the six years since the launch of Anonymous Operation Bahrain the hacktivists have inflicted hundreds of millions of dollars of damage both to the Bahrain government cyber-space, as well as peripheral targets such as the F1 races which directly benefit its largest investor, the "Royal" Family.

The bid to topple "King" Khalifa will end only with his exile, death, or imprisonment. But it started on February 15, 2011, two years ago as we pick up the story now, as part of the roll-out of a series of Anonymous Operations to support the "Arab Spring" uprisings that were spreading like a wildfire across the Middle East that were dubbed the *Freedom Operations*. As with all Anon Ops since those days, it started with a Press Release and video spread virally across the Internet. Anonymous was going after yet another dictator, this time - a "King".

Anonymous Press Release - Operation Bahrain

Tuesday - February 15, 2011

Dear Free-Thinking Citizens of THE WORLD --

The Bahrainian government has shown by its actions that it intends to brutally enforce its reign of injustice by limiting free speech and access to truthful information to its citizens and the rest of the world. It is time to call for an end to this oppressive regime. The most basic human right is the transparency of one's government, and Bahrain's is no exception. By interfering with the freedom to hold peaceful protests, the Bahraini government has made itself a clear enemy of its own citizens, and of Anonymous. The actions of this regime will not be forgotten, nor will they be forgiven.

When people are faced with such injustices, Anonymous hears those cries, and we will assist in bringing to justice those who commit criminal acts against the innocent. We will not remain silent and let these crimes against humanity continue.

The attempts to censor the Bahrainian people from the Internet - which prevents them from communicating their struggle to the outside world - are despicable strategies and show the cowardice of this regime, as well as the measures they are willing to take to cover their crimes.

To the people of Bahrain: We stand with you against your oppressors. This is not only your struggle, but one of people who are struggling for freedom all over the world. With the recent success in Tunisia and Egypt, we believe your revolution will succeed. Your brave actions will maintain the momentum of revolution for citizens all around the world wishing to regain their own freedoms.

We Are Anonymous

We Are Legion

We Do Not Forgive

We Do Not Forget

Expect Us

----------

Today OpNoPro and I were managing something truly rare, unique, historic, and epic. Something Anonymous had only successfully accomplished once before, in Syria. We were sending a small team of western hacktivists into Bahrain to visit several villages and assist activists, protester, and journalists, and human rights workers - in securing their communications with encryption and media organization to better project their messages to the world.

The small team of four included two European Anons, one American Anon, and a member of my own crew who was also American. They brought in with them laptops and a great deal of equipment, entering the country on a journalist visa posing as "YouTubers". It was the sort of crazy super dangerous human rights work that *Anonymous* has done more of than most, and for which we so seldom receive any credit for in main stream media. Only our big hacks are "sexy" enough for the news cycles. Backpacking over the Syrian border, or flying into Bahrain with a payload of illegal encryption software - these things some people would prefer to ignore when discussing *Anonymous*.

The team got through customs just fine, and OpNoPro and I began putting their adventure out on social media in real-time. Years later, many would still blame this decision, to not keep the mission secret until it was over - on what happened at the end. I feel compelled to say that the person from my crew, the one that was on the ground, who blamed me personally the loudest years later, was adamantly in favor of us journalizing their adventure for the world in real-time. Media is my expertise, but the media strategy for that mission was specifically approved by the entire ground team. The Europeans on the ground team found the whole drama amusing, and decided American activists need to man up and pay attention.

The Team's itinerary was no nonsense. There would be almost no video, recorded or streamed. The actual routes were secret and known only to the ground team. OpNoPro and I only knew of general villages they intended to try to get to. We had long since contacted activists in each village on the list, our crack team of western "hackers" were eagerly expected by local Bahrainis in each. Over the next many hours of blazingly hot daylight, our team was taxied in beat up old cars from village to village.

They had a prepared program of instruction, a couple of powerpoint and video presentations, pre-made software disks and thumb drives, and then whatever time was left before their ride got there to take them to the next village, they would devote to getting hospitality and answering questions. The plan only called for them to be on the ground in Manama for forty-eight hours, and there was no sleep at all scheduled. The plan was for them to sleep on the plane, coming and going - and not stop moving once they hit the ground. We actually hoped to cover ten main villages populated heavily by Shia Muslims, who were the biggest demographic amongst the pro-democracy protesters. They would succeed. But I get ahead of myself.

The rest of the day was a blur. OpNoPro and I had hung a huge color map of Manama on the wall of his living room, and drinking many pots of coffee, using the highly encrypted instant messager Jabber with  OTR, we followed the ground team from village to village, and reported on them and from them to social media and through that channel to the main stream media - who steadfastly refused to report on it. But the entire Anonymous Global Collective was following the action and making it viral. The world was watching. OpNoPro and I were determined to, in our small way - emulate the heroism of this ground team by not sleeping ourselves until tomorrow, when they would hopefully all get on flights home and it would be over.

----------

Sunday - February 17, 2013 approx. 8:30 PM ET  - "Safe House" Fredericton, New Brunswick - CANADA

As yet another winter snow storm piled more meters of the white stuff on top of us, an exhausted OpNoPro and I had finally tracked our ground team back to the airport in Manama. Time to quietly exit stage left, and get the fuck out of Dodge.

But it was not going to be that easy. There were two sets of checkpoints to get through in order to board. Our team made it through the first one in a mere ten minutes, and we were already getting ready to celebrate when the other shoe fell. Plain clothes police in suits came at our team from all directions in the lounge of the airport. The team leader was able to blast off a final series of tweets detailing the action as other team members ran interference for him by arguing with the police.

As OpNoPro and I sat there staring blankly at our screens in shock, the entire *Anonymous Global Collective* flew into a mindless panic wondering what they could do. But of course the answer for them was absolutely nothing, and we knew it - because it was our Op and we were totally helpless as well. We waited.... Four hours went by. Four *agonizing* hours. The first sign of life was an unintelligible and brief tweet. Our thought was it was the police messing with our team's mobile. But it was followed ten minutes later by more tweets. Our team had been released, and were boarding their respective flights. But they had been relieved of....everything, except the clothes on their backs. Even their luggage was seized and never returned.

----------

In retrospect analysis we discovered the likely reason our team was not immediately transported to a Bahrain prison or jail, as was the famous and award-winning investigative journalist Amber Lyon - was that it appears that that very day some big arms deal with the USA was on the line and waiting to be signed. In the interest of getting his guns and bombs with which he could continue to oppress and kill his own people, "King" Khalifa was more than happy to serve up the good will offering of a few well-meaning but misguided "hacktivists" from the West. We got amazingly, blindingly, lucky.

The seeds our team sowed in Bahrain continue to bear fruit to this day, where the pro-democracy resistance against the rule of "King" Khalifa continues un-abated - and utilizing the very tools we delivered to them those fateful days. Anonymous didn't come bearing money, weapons, food, or medicine. We came bearing something that in the end may be more valuable than any of those things in resisting Empire. We came bearing *information*.

----------

Monday - April 15, 2013 approx. 6:00 AM ET - "Safe House" Fredericton, New Brunswick - CANADA

Today, we were launching our second strike in what was becoming an annual ritual - the yearly attack on the F1 race in Manama. This was our third attack on the F1 in total, as related in my previous book - we also wrecked them badly in Montreal during the massive protests there in 2012. The misogynist bigoted prick who owned F1, one Bernie Ecclestone - was beginning to seriously hate *Anonymous*. Then again, after two years of relentless strikes - we weren't exactly favorites of the Bahrain Royal Family either. We openly called for Ecclestone and the Royal Family to share cells in the Hague together. OpNoPro and I were spending the morning blasting the Press Release and video to the mainstream media.

Anonymous Operation Bahrain Press Release: F1 To Be Targeted Again

Monday 15 April 2013

Greetings World --

We are Anonymous. And we have watched since the last Grand Prix F1 race in Manama, Bahrain.

Since last year, we have had millions of eyes trained on the continuing oppression of our freedom-loving brethren in Bahrain by the self-made "King" in Manama.

Since last year, when Anonymous in solidarity with hundreds of thousands of Bahraini – shut down the Grand Prix F1 race and said "no" to blood racing. One year since Anonymous dumped the personal information including credit card and passport numbers, of all the F1 attendees in Bahrain – and yet Bernnie Ecclestone and the "Royal Family" of Bahrain have learned nothing. So we are coming forward this year to wreck your little party again Mr. Ecclestone. Anonymous will not stand by and allow you a race fueled by the blood of our freedom loving comrades in Bahrain.

Beginning with the opening festivities of your little blood race, you can expect the presence of Anons from all over the globe inside your intertoobz. We will remove you from the world wide web, whether you be Grand Prix or Bahrain government – we shall take it all down. We will expose the personal data of any person who supports this race in any way. You have been warned. Once the festivities for this race begin in Bahrain, all bets are off. We call upon Bernie Ecclestone while there is still time; cancel your blood race now.

We Are Anonymous

We Are Legion

We Do Not Forgive

We Do Not Forget

Bernie Ecclestone & Bahrain Royal Family, it's too late to expect us!

----------

Around Noon things took an interesting turn when a hacker Crew from the Middle East contacted me and asked for a chat.

FreeBahrain: Thanks for speaking with me Commander X, it's an honor.

X: Just "X", please. What can I do for you?

FreeBahrain: I need you to announce an enforced boycott of the official F1 ticket and merchandise website. Tell anyone who makes a purchase that they will be punished by us dumping their credit card and other personal information.

X: Shit.....are you serious? That's pretty....extreme, don't you think.

FreeBahrain: Look, we got in and we're downloading the data now. We are dumping it, whether you warn people or not. Remember, we did it last time Ecclestone came here. We're serious.

X: Ok, ok - you got it. I'll put it out under the Anonymous flag as a warning, user beware.

OpNoPro and I spent the morning pushing out a Communique warning people not to buy from the F1 site. The amount of data that eventually ended up getting dumped this second time was a bit less damaging to end users than the previous year. But you had to brace up when doing hacktivism in the Middle East. These people faced serious and brutal tyranny, and they didn't play when it came to resistance!

As the day wore on, the above data dump was followed by a good half dozen defacements of fan related race websites. At least two dozen others were taken offline throughout the day by way of crowd-sourced DdoS attacks. In all, several tens of millions of dollars of damage was done in the course of four days of concerted attacks. Fuck Bernie Ecclestone.

----------

Wednesday - August 14, 2013 approx. 8:00 AM ET  - Starbucks Montreal, Quebec - CANADA

Having survived the winter in New Brunswick with OpNoPro, I said my good byes, making 'the old man' as he was known in Anonymous - an honorary Commander in the soon to be defunct *Peoples Liberation Front*. The *PLF* never really recovered internally from the stress of Operation Bahrain, and before the end of the year I would resolve to disband it as a no longer useful anachronism. I gave away some of the assets, and folded the rest into my new fledgling *Crew* I was forming called Legion Security. Meanwhile, I had relocated to Montreal via a brief visit with the Anon known as *Sage* in Quebec City, where I began the task of finally writing my first book, *Behind The Mask: An Inside Look At Anonymous*. I had actually had a title, cover, and a brief outline in my possession since I began this run in 2011. But I was finally attempting to find some spare time from either running from the law (or committing more cyber crimes to further piss them off) to work on actually writing down the story in my first tome.

Operationally within  Anonymous I had remained pretty focused on *Anonymous Operation Bahrain* throughout the late winter and spring, as the snow finally retreated and summer crept onto the scene. Summer in Montreal is about the happiest place a *crypto anarchist* like myself could imagine, especially for one living on the run as I was.

**83**

Today found me as usual, in a Starbucks and messing yet again with "King" Khalifa. Today, the activists across Bahrain had planned their annual Tamarrod Bahrain Action wherein they swarmed the streets and celebrated their peaceful revolution against their "King". I had spent the previous night up late preparing a special Press Release and video for Anonymous Operation Bahrain participation in cyber space.

Anonymous Operation Bahrain Press Release: Tamarrod Bahrain Action

Wednesday - August 14, 2013  6:30 AM ET USA

Greetings World --

We are Anonymous. We have been fighting along side our noble brothers and sisters in Bahrain now since February 2011. When the Saudi Troops came across the causeway to crush the courageous occupation at the now destroyed Pearl Roundabout, we were there to bear witness and help with media. When the self-proclaimed "King" of Bahrain ordered the arrest of doctors and nurses for treating protesters we attacked the government websites and servers in Bahrain relentlessly. When the human scum Bernie Ecclestone ran his blood race in Bahrain two years in a row, we wrecked the F1 Grand Prix sites and dumped the personal data of all who supported these blood races by purchasing tickets. Every day we monitor the ongoing protests in Bahrain, lending assistance where we can sometimes one individual at a time. We scan the Bahrain Internet, watching for any shutdown, interference - or attempts to surveil activists or journalists. We are gratified that our mask, the physical symbol of our movement has been outlawed in Bahrain. So long as the "King" reigns in Manama, and the people of Bahrain remain steadfast - we will never abandon our comrades.

Today, the Bahrain Resistance will begin a new phase of their rebellion: Tammarrod Bahrain. This afternoon Bahrain will be flooded with protesters for the Tamarrod Bahrain day. Bahrain's prime minister said on Monday his government would "forcefully confront" protests, and warned those behind planned demonstrations that they would be punished. This is unacceptable, undemocratic and we will not tolerate this. Anonymous will conduct the following action in support of Tammarod Bahrain:

1) Beginning at 1:00 PM ET USA Anonymous will launch a TwitterStorm to enlighten the world regarding the atrocities committed by the "King" of Bahrain.

2) Also beginning at 1:00 PM ET USA and running throughout the day, Anonymous will attack various websites of the regime and also of anyone who supports the regime. This may include western pr firms who are paid to white wash the crimes of the dictator in Manama.

These actions may include other activities not mentioned, as we will do whatever is necessary as the situation unfolds. We anticipate the protests will extend beyond today, and our action will continue for however long the Tammarod Bahrain movement sustains protests in the streets. Anonymous will never abandoned Bahrain. We encourage the media to follow the Twitter accounts mentioned on the bottom of this press release.

We call upon everyone outside of Bahrain to use their virtual skills to give Bahrainis their voice back. Bloggers, twitterians, facebookians, artists, hackers. To the brave and noble people of Bahrain: If you do not want to go to the streets get on the Internet. Contact us and let us know what is happening on the ground. Let us know the truth so we can spread it.

We stand by your side on this glorious day. Be brave dear friends, have no fear and know that we in Anonymous are with you always.

We Are Anonymous

We Are Everywhere

We Are Legion

We Do Not Forgive Tyranny

We Do Not Forget Crimes Against Humanity

To the "King" in Manama, your days are numbered - expect rebellion. Expect Tammarod. And Expect Anonymous

--------------------------------

Operation Bahrain - www.OperationBahrain.tk

Anonymous Global - www.AnonymousGlobal.org

Follow These Twitter Accounts For Updates:

@AnonymousWWN

@LegionSecGlobal

@OpBahrain_

@Anonymous_vii

----------

Once again we see the emergence of the information warfare tool Twitter Storm. For the past year we had seen a serious spike upwards in the effectiveness and reach of this strange social media platform, where you were constrained, among other things, to a mere one-hundred and forty characters per post. More and more it was apparent that he who ruled *Twitter* had the upper hand in many ways. The ability of a few activists to cause something as ephemeral as a *hashtag* to go viral around the world in minutes, and the fact that it will reach the ear of the powerful and elite - remains nothing short of astounding to me. While OpNoPro managed that effort and kept an eye on the IRC channels, I busied myself cataloging the many successful hacks and data dumps and pushed that ever growing list out to the media, giving many interviews along the way. It was all exhausting work.

----------

As the reader can tell by now I'm sure, I am very passionate about the situation in Bahrain. I have been obsessed with the freedom struggle there since I was part of the inception of *Anonymous Operation Bahrain* during the original *Freedom Operations* in 2011. Along the way I played a tiny roll in the making of the documentary movie *The Clouds Of Death* that showed the brutal over-use of CS tear gas (most of it from American manufacturers) that resulted in many deaths during the Bahrain Uprising. I've coordinated with Amber Lyon an award-winning investigative journalist formerly from CNN, and Barrett Brown wielding his *Project PM* to expose the PR firm *Qorvis*. Qorvis had targeted Amber herself for her critical media coverage of Bahrain. Here's a piece from Barrett's exhaustive investigation of them that relates to Bahrain as it remains published on Project PM:

Qorvis acquired its Bahrain account from Bell Pottinger in July 2010, for whom it served as a subcontractor until August 2011. In its November 2011 FARA statement, the firm declared having rendered the following services to the Kingdom:

monitoring daily media coverage relevant to Bahrain;

conducting press activities for government officials

drafting/distributing fact sheets, op-ed pieces speeches and news articles by e-mail in order to position Bahrain as a committed player in the war on terror, an agent of peace in the Middle East and other unspecified issues "pertinent to the Kingdom."

Service began approximately one month prior to a major crackdown on Shiite opposition figures and domestic media outlets. The New York Times speculated that the clampdown was part of the lead-up to the October 2010 parliamentary elections in which the Sunni establishment was expected to lose power to representatives of the Shiite demographic majority.

Qorvis sparked criticism in March, 2011, after issuing a misleading press release on behalf of the Bahraini government. After a draconian crackdown in which security forces in the Bahraini capital violently dispersed unarmed demonstrators, interrupted telecommunications services and reportedly hindered the treatment of injured civilians, Hilary Clinton issued a strong criticism of the government's actions. Qorvis responded by issuing a press release that emphasized Clinton's positive comments by presenting them out of context, while completely skirting her critical statements:

PARIS, March 19, 2011 /PRNewswire-USNewswire -- U.S. Secretary of State Hillary Rodham Clinton today emphasized the commitment of the United States toward Bahrain and her hope for the success of the National Dialogue in the island kingdom. She also affirmed the "sovereign right" of Bahrain to invite security forces from allied countries, and stated that the U.S. shared the goals of the GCC regarding Bahrain.

Since the uprising in Bahrain began, Bahrain's Crown Prince has called on all parties to engage in a dialogue to reconcile differences. Secretary Clinton said the goal of the United States is "a credible political process that can  address the legitimate aspirations of all the people of Bahrain."

Ambassador Houda Nonoo appreciated the Secretary's comments that dialogue should unfold in a peaceful, positive atmosphere that ensures that students can go to school, businesses can operate and people can undertake their normal daily activities. Said Ambassador Nonoo, "The government of Bahrain has consistently maintained that differences should be resolved peacefully around the negotiating table, but unfortunately, the opposition has not responded to this offer and instead has chosen to continue along the path of violence and disruption of normal life in Bahrain. It  is my government's belief that wisdom will prevail among the opposition and they will come to the negotiating table to  resolve all differences peacefully."

This has been issued by Qorvis Communications on behalf of the Embassy of the Kingdom of Bahrain to the United States.

SOURCE Embassy of the Kingdom of Bahrain to the United States*

Aside from misleading press releases and an incident described below involving activist Maryam al-Khawaja, the extent of Qorvis' role in the regime's managing of foreign perceptions may perhaps best be summed up via two specific incidents:

1. A 2012 event in D.C. in which three pro-regime youth were portrayed as embodying "the leading voice for change and reform" despite criticizing the more widespread opposition movement, and despite the event having been overseen by Qorvis and promoted by staffer Adam Croglia.

2. A 2012 Washington Post profile of Bahrain's ambassador to the U.S., Houda Nonoo, in which Nonoo consented to the interview only under the condition that a Qorvis representative would be in the room during its entirety.


Recent media:

'How Bahrain works Washington' from Salon (Dec 9, 2011)

'Meet Bahrain's Lobbyists' from The Hill (Dec 9, 2011)

Attack on Maryam al-Khawaja

In May, 2011, Bahrani human rights activist Maryam al-Khawaja was invited to speak as part of a panel discussion 'Dawn of a New Arab World' at the Oslo Freedom Forum. Writing in the Huffington Post, Oslo Freedom Forum founder and CEO Thor Halvorssen notes that 'the Bahraini government has been aided by a coterie of "reputation management" experts, including professionals from the Washington, D.C., offices of Qorvis Communications and the Potomac Square Group, in addition to Bell Pottinger out of their offices in London and Bahrain.' He goes on to describe:

'Within minutes of Maryam's speech (streamed live online) the global Bahraini PR machine went into dramatic overdrive. A tightly organized ring of Twitter accounts began to unleash hundreds of tweets accusing Maryam of being an extremist, a liar, and a servant of Iran. Simultaneously, the Oslo Freedom Forum's email account was bombarded with messages, all crudely made from a simple template, arguing that Maryam al-Khawaja is an enemy of the Bahraini people and a "traitor." Most of the U.S.-based fake tweeting, fake blogging (flogging), and online manipulation is carried out from inside Qorvis Communication's "Geo-Political Solutions" division.

The effort is mechanical and centrally organized, and it goes beyond the online world. In fact, right before Maryam was to give her speech, she noticed two young women in the crowd who stalk her speeches and heckled her a few days earlier at an event in the U.S. More so than intimidation, violence, and disappearances, the most important tool for dictatorships across the world is the discrediting of critics like Maryam.'

An earlier Huffington Post article on Qorvis, linked to by Halvorssen, states:

'One of the methods used by Qorvis and other firms is online reputation management -- through its Geo-Political Solutions (GPS) division, the firm uses '"black arts" by creating fake blogs and websites that link back to positive content, "to make sure that no one online comes across the bad stuff," says the former insider.

Other techniques include the use of social media, including Facebook, YouTube and Twitter.'

Attacks made on Maryam al-Khawaja through Twitter were numerous at that time and this, from @ActivateBahrain, is representative: #OFF2011 Maryam Al Khawaja is presenting a falsified presentation in #oslo about #Bahrain it is a package of lies and exaggerations.

Another, from @Dand00na86, and posted to the #Bahrain hashtag included two phone numbers and the message Let Maryam Al-Khawaja know what you think of her lies by calling her direct!

Thor Halvorssen also writes that a second Bahrani blogger, Ali Abdulemam, had also been invited to speak at the 2011 Forum:

'Ali was imprisoned by his government in September 2010 for "spreading false information." After being released on February 23, he enthusiastically accepted his speaking invitation and plans were made for his travel. And then he disappeared. No one has seen or heard from him since March 18.'

The Geo-Political Solutions division of Qorvis is under the supervision of partner Matt J Lauer.

----------

In an explosive turn of events, Amber Lyon would be fired from CNN and blow the whistle on them for accepting money in the form of paid broadcasting, as well as political pressure from the US State Dept., prompting CNN to bury and censor bad reporting on Bahrain and its "Royal Family".

Here's a brief snippet from the main piece that ran concordant with her revelation and leaking of documents regarding CNN's corrupt relationship with the Bahrain regime:

Despite Lyon's being stonewalled by CNNi, she said facts began emerging that shone considerable light on the relationship between the regime in Bahrain and CNNi when it came to "iRevolution". Upon returning from Bahrain in April, Lyon appeared on CNN several times to recount her own detention by security forces and to report on ongoing brutality by the regime against its own citizens, even including doctors and nurses providing medical aid to protesters. She said she did not want to wait for the documentary's release to alert the world to what was taking place.

In response, according to both the above-cited CNN employee and Lyon, the regime's press officers complained repeatedly to CNNi about Lyon generally and specifically her reporting for "iRevolution". In April, a senior producer emailed her to say:

"We are dealing with blowback from Bahrain govt on how we violated our mission, etc."

"It became a standard joke around the office: the Bahrainis called to complain about you again," recounted Lyon. Lyon was also told by CNN employees stationed in the region that "the Bahrainis also sent delegations to our Abu Dhabi bureau to discuss the coverage."

Internal CNN emails reflect continuous pressure on Lyon and others to include claims from the Bahraini regime about the violence in their country – even when, says Lyon, she knew first-hand that the claims were false.

One April 2011 email to Lyon from a CNN producer demands that she include in her documentary a line stating that "Bahrain's foreign minister says security forces are not firing on unarmed civilians," and another line describing regime claims accusing "activists like Nabeel Rajab of doctoring photos ... fabricating injuries".

Having just returned from Bahrain, Lyon says she "saw first-hand that these regime claims were lies, and I couldn't believe CNN was making me put what I knew to be government lies into my reporting."

----------

In addition, another journalist I deeply respect, and whom I've had the honor of meeting with - is Glenn Greenwald. He also has worked in lock step with Barrett Brown, Amber Lyon and me - to expose the many crimes of the Bahrain regime. Here's some of what he had to say in the Guardian in relation to Qorvis:

Spring, the regime undertook a massive, very well-funded PR campaign to improve its image. As reported by Bahrain Watch, the regime has spent more than $32m in PR fees alone since the commencement of the Arab Spring in February, 2011, including payments to some of Washington, DC's most well-connected firms and long-time political operatives, such as former Howard Dean campaign manager Joe Trippi.

One of the largest contracts the regime had was with the DC-based PR firm Qorvis Communications. As Time reported last November, the firm, which also does extensive PR work for Bahrain's close allies, the Saudi regime, "has a branch dedicated to rehabilitating the reputation of unsavory governments, a niche practice that has seen great demand in the wake of the Arab Spring".

Qorvis often led the way in complaining to CNNi about its Bahrain coverage. An internal email from CNN at the beginning of 2012, seen by the Guardian, records the firm's calling to complain about excessively favorable mentions of Nabeel Rajab, who had been arrested and charged over an anti-regime tweet, and was just this month sentenced to three years in prison for an "illegal demonstration".

The long-time CNN employee said that "iRevolution" was vetted far more heavily than the typical documentary:

"Because Amber was relatively new in reporting on the region, and especially because of the vocal complaints from the Bahrainis, the documentary was heavily scrutinized. But nobody could ever point to anything factually or journalistically questionable in Amber's reporting on Bahrain."

----------

One of the many consequences of *Anonymous Operation Bahrain* is there is a robust National Cell of the Global Collective called *Anonymous Bahrain,* consisting of many dedicated Bahraini hacktivists. They have been one of my most loyal allies in the years since we launched *Op Bahrain*, helping out on Ops from Montreal to Ferguson. They have been ever grateful not only for Anonymous' intervention early on, but for our ongoing attention and support. I can vouch that some of the most savvy hackers and courageous street activists and freedom fighters live in the tiny gulf nation of Bahrain.

"King" Khalifa has many powerful enemies among free thinking activists and journalists in the West. I have been privileged to work with the ones I've mentioned, as well as to know them all personally - and to do my part for the heroic *Bahrain Resistance*. I will never give up until Bahrain is free and "King" Khalifa and his line are gone.

# SIX

## *Operation Turkey*

-------------------

*"Right now, in more than 60 cities of the country, there are more than a hundred demonstrations, bringing together more than three million people. Three days ago, 700 people gathered to protest this, and police gassed them. Next day, 7,000 people gathered in the same square, and the police gassed them. And on Saturday, 700,000 people came together, and then the police fled."*

~~ Professor Koray Caliskan

• • •

Sunday - June 1, 2014 approx. 8:00 AM ET - Starbucks Montreal, Quebec - CANADA

In order to understand the street revolution in Turkey that began in Gezi Park, you have to understand the genesis - the cathartic moment that began a cascade of historic events that are still unfolding in Turkey even to this day. Not, perhaps the way everyone hoped or thought it might back when we pick up the tale of *Anonymous Operation Turkey* in 2014. And *Anonymous* was there from day one, thanks in part to an already very active domestic cell in country called *Anonymous Turkey*. One year ago today, to be exact - on June 1st of 2013, we started *Anonymous Operation Turkey*. I know, because I helped the *Anons* in Turkey launch the Op. It was a great honor that they asked me not only to help, but to assist in leading - this amazing *Freedom Operation*. And it all began, as the *Lorax* would say, with the trees....

The initial cause of the protests was the plan to remove Gezi Park, one of the few remaining green spaces in the center of the European side of Istanbul. The plan involved pedestrianising Taksim Square and rebuilding the Ottoman-era Taksim Military Barracks, which had been demolished in 1940. Development projects in Turkey involve "cultural preservation boards" which are supposed to be independent of the government, and in January such a board rejected the project as not serving the public interest. However a higher board overturned this on May 1st, in a move park activists said was influenced by the government. The ground floor of the rebuilt barracks was expected to house a shopping mall, and the upper floors luxury flats, although in response to the protests the likelihood of a shopping mall was downplayed, and the possibility of a museum raised. The main contractor for the project is the Kalyon Group, described in 2013 by the BBC as "a company which has close ties with the governing Justice and Development (AK) Party".

The Gezi Park protests began in April, having started with a petition in December 2012.

The protests were renewed on May 27th, culminating in the creation of an encampment occupying the park. A raid on this encampment on May 29th prompted outrage and wider protests. Although Turkey has a history of police brutality, the attack on a peaceful sit-in by environmentalists was different enough to spur wider outrage than such previous incidents, developing into the largest protests in Turkey in decades. The large number of trees that were cut in the forests of northern Istanbul for the construction of the Yavuz Sultan Selim Bridge (Third Bosphorus Bridge) and the new Recep Tayyip Erdoğan International Airport (the world's largest airport, with a capacity for 150 million passengers per year) were also influential in the public sensitivity for protecting Gezi Park. According to official Turkish government data, a total of 2,330,012 trees have been cut for constructing the Erdoğan Airport and its road connections; and a total of 381,096 trees have been cut for constructing the highway connections of the Yavuz Sultan Selim Bridge; reaching an overall total of 2,711,108 trees which were cut for the two projects.

A wave of demonstrations and civil unrest in Turkey began on May 28, 2013, initially to contest the urban development plan for Istanbul's Taksim Gezi Park. The protests were sparked by outrage at the violent eviction of a sit-in at the park protesting the plan, where young activists had quite literally chained themselves to the trees in an effort to prevent them being cut down by construction crews. Subsequently, supporting protests and strikes took place across Turkey, protesting a wide range of concerns at the core of which were issues of freedom of the press, of expression, assembly, and the government's encroachment on Turkey's secularism. With no centralized leadership beyond the small assembly that organized the original environmental protest, the protests have been compared to the Occupy movement and the May 1968 events in the USA. As with all the previous *Arab Spring* street uprisings, social media played a key part in these protests - not least because much of the Turkish media downplayed the protests, particularly in the early stages.

Three and a half million people (out of Turkey's population of 80 million) are estimated to have taken an active part in almost 5,000 demonstrations across Turkey connected with the original Gezi Park protest. Eleven people were eventually killed, including one Anon, and more than eight-thousand were injured, many critically. The following is a timeline of the historic Gezi Park Uprising:

2013 May On the morning of May 28th, around 50 environmentalists are camping out in Gezi Park in order to prevent its demolition. The protesters initially halt attempts to bulldoze the park by refusing to leave.

Police use tear gas to disperse the peaceful protesters and burn down their tents in order to allow the bulldozing to continue. Photos of the scene, such as an image of a young female protester (later nicknamed the "woman in red") holding her ground while being sprayed by a policeman, quickly spread throughout the world media. The Washington Post reports that the image "encapsulates Turkey's protests and the severe police crackdown", while Reuters calls the image an "iconic leitmotif".

The size of the protests grows

Police raid the protesters' encampments. Online activists' calls for support against the police crackdown increase the number of sit-in protesters by the evening.

Police carry out another raid on the encampment in the early morning of May 31, using water cannons and tear gas to disperse the protesters to surrounding areas and setting up barricades around the park to prevent re-occupation. Throughout the day, the police continue to fire tear gas, pepper spray and water cannons at demonstrators, resulting in reports of more than 100 injuries.

MP Sırrı Süreyya Önder and journalist Ahmet Şık were hospitalized after being hit by tear gas canisters.

The executive order regarding the process decided earlier had been declared as "on-hold".

10,000 gather in Istiklal Avenue. According to Governor Hüseyin Avni Mutlu, 63 people are arrested and detained. Police use of tear gas is criticized for being "indiscriminate". The interior minister, Muammer Guler, says the claims of the use of disproportionate force would be investigated.

2013 June Heavy clashes between protesters and police continue until early morning around İstiklal Avenue. Meantime, around 5,000 people gather at the Asian side of İstanbul and march through Kadıköy Bağdat Avenue. Around 1,000 people continue to march towards the European side and they cross the Bosphorus Bridge on foot. Protesters reach Beşiktaş in the morning and police disperse them with tear gas.

Clashes continue throughout the day. Republican People's Party leader Kemal Kılıçdaroğlu announce that they will move their planned rally to Taksim Square instead of Kadıköy. Prime Minister Recep Tayyip Erdoğan says he has approved that decision. Around 15:45 police forces retreat from Taksim Square. Thousands of protesters gather at Gezi Park and Taksim Square.

Protester Ethem Sarısülük gets shot in the head by a riot policeman during the protests at Ankara Kizilay Square. He dies 14 days later due to his injuries.

Prime Minister Recep Tayyip Erdoğan describes the protesters as "a few looters" in a televised interview. He also criticizes social media, calling Twitter a "menace" and an "extreme version of lying".

At night, police forces try to disperse protesters gathered in the Beşiktaş district. Clashes between police and protesters continue until next morning. Beşiktaş football team supporter group Çarşı members hijack a bulldozer and chase police vehicles.

Front side of AKM (Atatürk Cultural Center) building at Taksim Square gets covered with banners.

In Ankara, police tries to disperse thousands of protesters who are attempting to march on the prime minister's office there.

PM Recep Tayyip Erdoğan speaks to reporters at the airport before leaving for a three-day trip to North Africa. He threatens the protesters saying "We are barely holding the 50 percent (that voted for us) at home".

Turkey's deputy prime minister Bulent Arinc offers an apology to protesters.

June 22 year Abdullah Cömert dies after being hit in the head by tear gas canister during the protests at Hatay.

PM Recep Tayyip Erdoğan speaks to his supporters outside of İstanbul Atatürk Airport on his return from a four-day trip to North Africa. Erdoğan blames "interest rate lobbies" claiming they are behind Gezi protests. His supporters chant "Give us the way, we will crush Taksim Square".

Riot police forces enter Taksim Square early in the morning. They make announcements that they will not be entering Gezi Park and their mission is to open Taksim Square to traffic again. Most protesters gather at Gezi Park, but a small group carrying banners of the Socialist Democracy Party retaliate using molotov cocktails and slingshots.

Some people like Luke Harding from The Guardian claims that undercover police threw molotov cocktails, "staging a not very plausible 'attack' on their own for the benefit of the cameras". These claims were rejected by the governor of Istanbul, Hüseyin Avni Mutlu.

After police tries to enter Gezi park, clashes continue throughout the night and CNN International makes an eight-hour live coverage. Pro-government media accuses CNN and Christiane Amanpour of deliberately showing Turkey in a state of civil war.

PM Recep Tayyip Erdoğan holds a meeting with the members of Taksim Solidarity in Ankara. When a member says that those protests have a sociological aspect, he gets angry and leaves the meeting saying "We are not going to learn what sociology is from you!".

Justice and Development Party party organizes a mass rally called "Respect to National Will" in Ankara. Talking at the rally, PM Recep Tayyip Erdoğan says that "If protesters don't move out of Gezi Park, police forces will intervene".

At about 17:30, Police forces begin making announcments to protesters telling to leave Gezi Park. Police forces make an assault about 20:50 and clear Gezi Park. Protesters move to areas around İstiklal Street and clash with police.

Meanwhile, about 5,000 protesters gather at the Asian side of İstanbul and begin marching towards the European side. Riot police forces disperse the protesters with tear gas before reaching the Bosphorus Bridge.

Heavy clashes between police and protesters continue until morning at various parts of İstanbul.

Justice and Development Party organizes its second rally at İstanbul Kazlıçeşme Square.

A general strike and protests organized by five trade unions take place in almost every part of Turkey. Strikes doesn't have any negative effect on the daily life which led criticism of unions and their power.

The "Standing Man", Erdem Gündüz starts his silent protest in the evening. Similar protests consisting of simply stopping and standing still spread everywhere in Turkey.

President Abdullah Gül announces suspension of Gezi Park redevelopment plans.

An investigation regarding police brutality is opened and some officers dismissed

Violence and mass demonstrations spread again in the country, after police attacks on thousands of protesters who threw carnations at them and called for brotherhood. Mass demonstrations occur again in Taksim Square, Istanbul and also in Güvenpark and Dikmen in Ankara to protest against the release of police officer Ahmet Şahbaz who fatally shot Ethem Sarısuluk in the head, as well as against events in Lice, Diyarbakır and Cizre, Şırnak. Riot police suppress the protesters partially with plastic bullets and some tear gas bombs and some protesters are detained. There is also a major police intervention in Ankara. The Istanbul LGBT Pride 2013 parade at Taksim Square attracts almost 100,000 people.

Participants were joined by Gezi Park protesters, making the 2013 Istanbul Pride the biggest pride ever held in Turkey and eastern Europe. The European Union praises Turkey that the parade went ahead without disruption.

July 2013 A machete-wielding man attacks the Gezi Park protesters at Taksim Square. He is detained by the police, but gets released the same day. After being released, he flees to Morocco on 10 July.

Thousands of people stage the "1st Gas Man Festival" (1. Gazdanadam Festivali) in Kadıköy to protest against the police crackdown on anti-government and nature-supporting demonstrations across the country. With the arrival of Ramadan, protesters in Istanbul hold mass iftar (the ceremonial meal breaking the daily fast) for all comers. 19-year-old Ali İsmail Korkmaz, who was in a coma since 4 June dies. He was severely battened by a group of casually dressed people on June 3rd while running away from police intervention.

2013 August The scale and frequency of demonstrations die down in the summer. Human chains are organized for peace and against intervention in Syria. Protesters begin painting steps in rainbow colors.

----------

The sit-in at Taksim Gezi Park was restored after police withdrew from Taksim Square on June 1st, and developed into an Occupy-like camp, with thousands of protesters in tents, organizing a library, medical center, food distribution, and their own media. This was the day that *Anonymous Operation Turkey* was launched, with the usual video and Press Release:

Anonymous Operation Turkey - Press Release

Saturday - June 1, 2013  10:30 PM ET USA

Greetings World --

We are Anonymous. And we have watched for days with horror as our brothers and sisters in Turkey who are peacefully rising up against their tyrannical government have been brutalized, beaten, run over with riot vehicles, shot with water cannons and gassed in the streets. From the epicenter of their revolution in Taksim Square to every city in Turkey, the people have risen. Hundreds of thousands have taken and held the streets for days, despite the relentless assault of the police. Thousands have been arrested.

Turkey is supposed to be a so called "modern" democracy, but the Turkish government behaves like the petty dictators in China or Iran. Anonymous is outraged by this behavior, and we will unite across the globe and bring the Turkish government to its knees. We will attack every internet and communications asset of the Turkish government. You have censored social media and other communications of your people in order to suppress the knowledge of your crimes against them. Now Anonymous will shut you down, and your own people will remove you from power. Let the "Turkish Summer" begin!

We Are Anonymous

We Are Everywhere

We Are Legion

We Do Not Forgive

We Do Not Forget

Government of Turkey, it is too late to EXPECT US

-------------------------------------------------

Anonymous Op Turkey Website - www.OperationTurkey.tk

Anonymous Op Turkey Video - https://vimeo.com/213856218

Anonymous Turkey - anonsturkey.blogspot.de

Anonymous Global - www.AnonymousGlobal.org

Legion Security- www.LegionSecurity.cf

RedHack - redhack.tumblr.com

----------

After the Gezi Park camp was cleared by riot police on June 15th, protesters began to meet in other parks all around Turkey and organized public forums to discuss ways forward for the protests. Turkish Prime Minister Recep Tayyip Erdoğan dismissed the protesters as "a few looters" on June 2nd. Police suppressed the protests with tear gas and water cannons. In addition to the 11 deaths and over 8,000 injuries, more than 3,000 arrests were made. Excessive use of force by police and the overall absence of government dialogue with the protesters was criticized by some foreign countries and international organizations.

The range of the protesters was described as being broad, encompassing both right- and left-wing individuals.

Their complaints ranged from the original local environmental concerns to such issues as the authoritarianism of Recep Tayyip Erdoğan, curbs on alcohol, a recent row about kissing in public, and the war in Syria. Protesters called themselves çapulcu (looters), reappropriating Erdoğan's insult for themselves (and coined the derivative "chapulling", given the meaning of "fighting for your rights"). Many users on Twitter also changed their screen name and used çapulcu instead. According to various analysts, the protests are the most challenging events for Erdoğan's ten-year term and the most significant nationwide disquiet in decades.

The Justice and Development Party (AKP) led by Recep Tayyip Erdoğan has governed since 2002, winning the 2002, 2007 and 2011 elections by large margins. Under its rule the economy of Turkey recovered from the 2001 financial crisis and recession, driven in particular by a construction boom. At the same time, particularly since 2011, it has been accused of driving forward an Islamist agenda, having undermined the secularist influence of the Turkish Army. During the same period it also increased a range of restrictions on human rights, most notably freedom of speech and freedom of the press, despite improvements resulting from the accession process to the European Union.

Since 2011, the AKP has increased restrictions on freedom of speech, freedom of the press, Internet use, television content, and the right to free assembly. It has also developed links with Turkish media groups, and used administrative and legal measures (including, in one case, a $2.5 billion tax fine) against critical media groups and journalists: "over the last decade the AKP has built an informal, powerful, coalition of party-affiliated businessmen and media outlets whose livelihoods depend on the political order that Erdoğan is constructing.

Those who resist do so at their own risk". The government has been seen by certain constituencies as increasingly Islamist and authoritarian, An education reform strengthening Islamic elements and courses in public primary and high schools was approved by the parliament in 2012, with Erdoğan saying that he wanted to foster a "pious generation". The sale and consumption of alcohol in university campuses has been banned. People have been given jail sentences for blasphemy.

While construction in Turkey has boomed and has been a major driver for the economy, this has involved little to no local consultation. For example, major construction projects in Istanbul have been "opposed by widespread coalitions of diverse interests. Yet in every case, the government has run roughshod over the projects' opponents in a dismissive manner, asserting that anyone who does not like what is taking place should remember how popular the AKP has been when elections roll around." Corruption concerns have also been raised, particularly relating to the Kanal İstanbul. Environmental issues, especially since the 2010 decision of the government to build additional nuclear power plants and the third bridge, led to continued demonstrations in Istanbul and Ankara. The Black Sea Region has seen dozens of protests against the construction of waste-dumps, nuclear and coal power plants, mines, factories and hydroelectric dams. 24 local musicians and activists in 2012 created a video entitled "Diren Karadeniz" ("Resist, Black Sea"), which prefigured the ubiquitous Gezi Park slogan "Diren Gezi".

The government's stance on the civil war in Syria is another cause of social tension in the country. Controversy within progressive communities has been sparked by plans to turn Turkey's former Christian Hagia Sophia churches (now museums) in Trabzon and possibly Istanbul into mosques, a plan which failed to gain the support of prominent Muslim leaders from Trabzon. In 2012 and 2013, structural weaknesses in Turkey's economy were becoming more apparent.

Economic growth slowed considerably in 2012 from 8.8% in 2011 to 2.2% in 2012 and forecasts for 2013 were below trend. Unemployment remained high at at least 9% and the current account deficit was growing to over 6% of GDP. A key issue Erdoğan campaigned for prior to the 2011 election was to rewrite the military-written constitution from 1982. Key amongst Erdoğan's demands were for Turkey to transform the role of President from that of a ceremonial role to an executive presidential republic with emboldened powers and for him to be elected president in the 2014 presidential elections. To submit such proposals to a referendum needs 330 out of 550 votes in the Grand National Assembly and to approve without referendum by parliament requires 367 out of 550 votes (a two-thirds majority) - The AKP currently holds only 326 seats. As such the constitutional commission requires agreement from opposition parties, namely the CHP, MHP and BDP who have largely objected to such proposals. Moreover, the constitutional courts have ruled that current President Abdullah Gül is permitted to run for the 2014 elections, who is widely rumored to have increasingly tense relations and competition with Erdoğan. Furthermore, many members of parliament in the governing AKP have internally also objected by arguing that the current presidential system suffices. Erdoğan himself is currently barred from running for a fourth term as prime minister in the 2015 general elections due to current AKP by-laws, largely sparking accusations from the public that Erdoğan's proposals were stated in light of him only intending to prolong his rule as the most dominant figure in politics. The constitutional proposals have mostly so far been delayed in deliberations or lacked any broad agreement for reforms, but they were finally passed in their entirety in 2017 as this book goes to print.

----------

One of the most historic things to come from *Anonymous Operation Turkey* in my opinion was an alliance formed between my *Crew*, *Anonymous*, and a fifteen year old hacktivist *Crew* from Turkey called *RedHack*. There is a documentary with English subtitles floating around the Internet, and I can not suggest highly enough that the reader check it out. Founded in 1995, they were contemporary with the PLF/Legion Sec and predated *Anonymous* by a decade. These hackers were serious business, and an original part of the *Hacker Undrground*.

*RedHack* (Kızıl Hackerlar or Kızıl Hackerlar Birliği), is a Turkish Marxist-Leninst computer hacker group founded in 1995. The group has claimed responsibility for hacking institutions which include the Council of Higher Education, Turkish police forces, the Turkish Army, Türk Telekom, and the National Intelligence Organization and many other websites. The group's core membership is said to number twelve; the leader's pseudonym is MaNYaK. RedHack is the first hacker group which has been accused of being a terrorist organization and is currently one of the world's most wanted hacker groups.

In their 25 years of operation, the hacktivist group RedHack has pulled off many high-profile strikes, such as leaking documents from Turkish National Police, penetrating the Turkish army's Commando Brigade, wiping out electricity bills in protest of a power plant, and defacing milk companies that delivered tainted milk in primary schools. But most of their activities go unreported in Turkey's censored media, which aims to hide the government corruption and incapacity RedHack often reveals. In an epic online meeting this past winter at OpNoPro's house, he bore witness to the formation of an alliance facilitated by my *Crew* between *RedHack* and *Anonymous*. In 2016 *RedHack* gave the Daily Dot an extensive interview. A brief excerpt from that interview can be useful in revealing RedHack's general philosophy, especially as it relates to other elements in the *Hacker Underground*.

Daily Dot: Why did you hack Berat Albayrak's email accounts? Why him in particular?

RedHack: We were tracking Berat Albayrak for some time. He was our target because we believed that he maintained the dirty relationships of the party in power, especially with his career that spans from his education inside the Gülen Movement to his rise within Turkey's Justice and Development Party [formerly led by Erdoğan, known by its Turkish acronym, AKP].

Daily Dot: There is the fact that Turkey's Energy Ministry was using U.S.-based companies' email services, without encryption on emails or sensitive documents, and that NSA and U.S. courts could access this information. What sort of security failures do these point out?

RedHack: This is very important. We noticed the same when we hacked Minister of Interior, Muammer Güler, previously. A lot can be said about the practice of keeping all the secret correspondence of the government, also the links of the corrupted network that they themselves are in, over U.S.-based means of communication. But let us summarize in one word: "incapacity."

From the email correspondences, and our 'visits' to his computers, we can say that if there would be a merit-based appointment system in Turkey, even the President would not be trusted with a light switch; they would probably leave the lights on all night.

Daily Dot: How would you define your own acts? Do you agree that they are illegal, or do you think they are legitimate because they are political?

RedHack: Certainly we are not bound by the laws of thieves, murderers and fascists who burned people in basements.

[Note: This refers to the 'Cizre Massacre']. We do not care about the decrees they issue about us, we do not even take Erdoğan and his security forces seriously. Public interest and the history of the revolutionary struggle provide legitimacy to our actions. Let us also add this: While we try to do our best with our acts and our statements, sometimes this does not happen. But the people should not doubt our aims and the faith we have for the struggle.

There are other active hacker groups, some nationalists, others closer to the government. At times, they perform hacks of political nature as well, such as recent examples of attacks to pro-Kurdish party, Peoples' Democratic Party [known by its Turkish acronym, HDP], leaking their private conversations. Do you find this legitimate?

While these acts would be considered political, they are never legitimate. The groups you mentioned have switched sides; even their friends question their legitimacy now. We find it a waste of time to talk about them.

Daily Dot: After your ultimatum to the government, were you hopeful that dissidents would be released, or did you make that statement to draw attention to their case?

RedHack: Of course we try to raise public awareness against the attacks of fascists; and we can say we are at least partially successful in this. Right on this point, the difference between hacking and hacktivism becomes visible. We are hacktivists!

Let's build propositions on the philosophy of hactivism; one can say that hacktivist actions have not only a political meaning, but also that they are the voice of the oppressed and the excluded. This is what defines the hactivist character of the RedHack. We are actually not hackers, we are hacktivists!

Daily Dot: The Twitter accounts that you used to announce your actions are suspended by Twitter. It is against the rules of Twitter to share personal information, but Twitter did not suspend other accounts of a similar political nature, including WikiLeaks, Guccifer 2.0, TheCthulhu and Phineas Fisher. Do you think Twitter's censorship is also political, do you think Turkey pressures the company to censor you?

RedHack: All social media companies and all spaces of information sharing, including Twitter, are owned by the hegemons. Their understanding of freedom is not defined by the truth, but is limited by the threats to their hegemony. Let alone personal data, Twitter allows ISIS members who behead people, and pedophiles, too. We do not expect Twitter to let this corrupt network to be revealed as such. But we trust upon the opposition journalists whose principles are based on liberty and facts. Being among their readers, we are certain that they will not mislead us, they never did.

Daily Dot: Why did you limit access to Albayrak's email archive only to the journalists, initially?

RedHack: We have conducted similar hacks before. We are Socialists, and our acts can only serve as the tools of a political struggle. Sometimes we hear so many people saying "Release it all! Are you bargaining with them? Why don't you release all the information?"

We have seen all of the immoral and crooked relations that these people in power have built upon. But we are not paparazzi. We are Marxists who put up a struggle in a Leninist organizational structure. In the emails, there could be content of private sort, but we cannot release those for the tabloids. When we filter out all such material, we will release the whole archive to the public for our strong belief in the freedom of information, and public's right to know.

Daily Dot: When daily Evrensel's reporter Cemil Uğur was jailed, you threatened to release the material to the public "unfiltered," and you did so on Oct. 8. Even if the cloud services were promptly blocked, hundreds of people downloaded the whole archive via torrent. Did you change your mind about filtering?

RedHack: No, personal photographs are filtered out. These were also not provided in the leak to the journalists. As Socialists, we cannot take part in immoral acts.

But some people who downloaded the archive found email receipts from Amazon that are certainly related to his private life. How do you explain this?

We did our best to filter the emails in order to refrain from publishing the content that is of tabloid nature. We had filtered pictures of his wife, and certain correspondence he had. This shows of sensitivity regarding this matter. However, the pressure from the party in power and the 17.3GB size of the data seemingly prevented us from completing this task.

Our opposition is built upon political awareness and action capacities, not on bedroom moralities. It is unfortunate that public's interest is currently focused on this. But they should instead demand accountability on ISIS oil trade that finances terrorism, and unjustified appointments of public employees.

Daily Dot: How do you choose the journalists you provide access to? What do you expect from them in return?

RedHack: Frankly, the public chooses these journalists, and these journalists make choices in their own will.

The main dynamic of this relationship is their libertarian attitude, their choices to report about the oppressed and excluded groups, and the public's respect to their work. Therefore, it's not a difficult selection. We were never wrong. There are journalists with whom we lost contact because of suspended accounts; we hope they don't resent us because of this. Under such heavy censorship and fascist attacks, these are probable outcomes.

Daily Dot: Why did you feel the need to hack daily Sözcü's website and publish your own news article? Don't you think it also puts pressure on the journalists to cover your story? Will you hack other outlets as well if they also fail to cover it?

RedHack: Daily Sözcü's recent editorial line was too much of a police mouthpiece. We think our act was not only a warning but also a way to inform the people in the opposition who read daily Sözcü. However, not every hack is an aggression, this was a hack but not an attack. One should think of this as a penetration test, we just reported it in our own way.

Daily Dot: How about a pro-government hacker group publishing a piece at an opposition daily? Would this also be a legitimate political act?

RedHack: This question is similar to the one you asked above: Political acts and legitimate acts are different. Legitimate political acts cannot be against people, against those who support the oppressed. Of course, the definition of legitimacy is divisive on its own. But we would never approve actions against Socialist organizations that work for the rights of the people, we define such acts as "fascist attacks."

Daily Dot: Do you think there are limitations, censorship and self-censorship, about the reporting of your actions?

RedHack: The general public started to hear more about us from 2012 onwards, thanks to the social media and the new means of communication, but we have accomplished many sensational hacks since 1997. So, one can easily say that we have been under censorship for the last 20 years. But this is not different from the censorship on other socialist organizations, and the independent press; their struggle went underreported just like ours. This is because the media falls under the hegemon class. Today, where thieves, rapists, and child abusers receive high honors, we would question ourselves if we wouldn't be censored.

Daily Dot: How do you evaluate your recent hack? Do you think it accomplished its aims?

RedHack: There are three stages of hacktivist acts:

1. Planning and attack
2. Propaganda and accountability
3. Retreat

We are at the second stage. All this censorship and blocking indicates that we were successful, but it would be too early to say it before it ends. When those whom the government took for being "RedHack members" are liberated from fascists, we can talk about this at a party. ☐ ☐

Lawyers of those seven people in police custody claimed that their clients were ill-treated and tortured. All suspects were later released due to lack of evidence. But before that, you released a very detailed statement about how you performed the Albayrak hack, starting from back in June. Was it to prove that those in custody are not the RedHack members?

The only thing the police had on them is an anonymous tip. We have absolutely no idea why these people were suspected to be linked to us. From what we have read so far, we understand that those detained share a similar worldview with us, but that's all. It does not make any sense to detain same group of people after every RedHack action. Fascism makes no sense, that's obvious, but we think that they try to intimidate the public this way, to force the public to self-censorship. And we believe police, too, are aware that this intimidation will not work.

Daily Dot: How do you think you contribute to the opposition groups in Turkey with these actions? And what is your ultimate target—under which type of political regime would the RedHack stop its actions?

RedHack: The founding philosophy of The RedHack is opening a digital propaganda space to the opposition groups. Therefore, RedHack is an online "self-defence movement" of the oppressed. While our action capabilities seem to popularize us, as a significant power of self-defence, we will never get spoiled by our popularity.

We are perceived to act mainly for the Socialist struggle inside Turkey, but actually we are putting up a global struggle. We are much [more] widely known in the world than in Turkey. And we will keep this struggle until the beauty rules the world, because "Beauty will save the world."

----------

In October of 2013 when the Turkish government threatened *RedHack* with prosecution in retaliation for their actions against them, Anonymous released the following Communique on behalf of the *Global Collective*:

Anonymous Communique: Operation Turkey & RedHack Alliance

Saturday - October 5, 2013

Hello Turkish Government --

We are Anonymous.

It has come to our attention that you are preparing to include the RedHack Team into the "Terror Organizations" list.

The Socialist group RedHack brought down the Turkish Foreign Ministry website yesterday morning, replacing its contents with pictures showing the Turkish prime minister embracing former Libyan dictator Mummar Gaddafi and Syrian President Bashar al-Assad: "Ministry of War and Slavery, not Foreign Affairs." A caption for the pictures read: "Brothers yesterday, enemies today"

Koru admitted the incident was due to a "weakness of security". Seven people who are suspected of being members of RedHack are already under arrest.
The investigation into the group has reached a critical position.

The prosecutor who is already conducting a comprehensive investigation into the group, are preparing to include them into the "Terror Organizations" list. Prosecution Office confirmed in his report to the Anti-Terror Branch, that the group has a Marxist-Leninist manifesto. He has consulted the Anti-Terror branch if this group can be treated within the penal code as a terror organization.

The RedHack team said:

Bro we are not worried about being arrested or killed, we think we still got lot to offer to the people of Turkey. That's why we are worried. if we are wiped out this people will continue to suffer under the current fascist regime . At least now they see a hope in us. The people still need us.

The RedHack group are not sure of what the next few hours or days will hold for them.

We demand the cessation of these illegitimate attacks against RedHack. We demand the immediate release of innocent people who have nothing to do with RedHack.

We demand the cessation of these operations to instill fear into those who work to uncover truth. Anonymous will support RedHack, and everyone working in Turkey to tear down barriers to free information, until the end.

This support, we will show in every way we possess.
An attack on Redhack is an attack on free information, a free press, free expression and on Anonymous!

We Are Anonymous

We Are Legion

We Do Not Forgive

We Do Not Forget

Expect Us

----------

The entire top echelon of leadership for *RedHack*, my entire *Crew* including OpNoPro, and few influential *Anons* - were present in the encrypted chat when this historic alliance was formed. It was weighty indeed to meet hacking legends the likes of MaNYaK and his also famous 'lieutenants' in *RedHack*. The meeting lasted several hours, and resulted, in addition to a better solidifying of the relationship RedHack had with WikiLeaks, a perpetual and unbreakable bond between *RedHack* and the western hacktivists in the *Anonymous Global Collective*.

Today's action was to celebrate the one year anniversary of *Anonymous Operation Turkey* by helping *RedHack* deliver yet another leak to WikiLeaks, and to facilitate the propagation of that leak into Turkey. Beyond our usual propaganda role, we were also helping distribute instructions and tools to Turkish people to assist them in circumventing the Turkish government's perennial attempts to censor *RedHack* leaks. Since the protests across the nation had begun to dwindle now at the one year mark, the majority of *Anonymous* effort in *Operation Turkey* was geared toward honing our anti-censorship skills by practicing them on the Turkish government. *RedHack* had long since picked up all the hacking work in the Op, leaving us free to help keep information flowing into and out of Turkey via the Internet.

----------

Monday - November 17, 2014 approx. 8:30 AM ET  - Starbucks Montreal, Quebec - CANADA

So many times in *Anonymous* I have been asked, "why don't you hack into banks and delete all our debt?". This has become a more frequent question, especially since the advent of the television series *Mr. Robot* - which has as it's storyline just such a premise. The short answer is, we do this all the time.

The most notable example in my books would be the story of *Lulzmas* mentioned in *Behind The Mask: An Inside Look At Anonymous*, in which the Anonymous hacking Crew AntiSec used credit card data stolen from the private intelligence firm *Stratfor* to make nearly one million dollars in donations to non-profits on Christmas Day 2011. Today would be yet another classic, epic, and historic example of what we call in the business a *Robinhood Hack*.

In one of the most epic hacks I have ever had the honor of witnessing and being a part of, *RedHack* had hacked into the state-owned utility company and had permanently deleted approximately six-hundred and seventy *billion* dollars in past bills. They also deleted all the backups. Essentially, if you owed the Turkish government money for electricity when you went to sleep that Friday, you woke up this Monday morning with that entire debt irrevocably gone. Thanks to the hackers. It was an almost *unspeakable* blow to the government's finances, and hugely embarrassing for what was increasing becoming a full blown dictatorship in Turkey.

My *Crew* and *Anonymous* had coordinated ahead of time with elements of *RedHack* to give the hack as much global publicity as possible. 2014 had essentially turned into the year of *RedHack* and *Anonymous Operation Turkey* for me. RedHack was already a legend around the world, and beloved by the people in Turkey. Today, they went from being legends to myths in their own lifetimes. And it is well earned, they are all heroes.

# SEVEN

## *Operation Ferguson*

-----------------------

*"This ain't your Daddy's civil rights movement. We ain't ashamed to be angry because we're supposed to be angry. They're killing us, and that's the bottom line."*

~~ Tef Poe

Sunday - August 9, 2014 approx. 1:00 PM ET - Starbucks Montreal, Quebec - CANADA

It was a lazy summer Sunday in Montreal, which means for me and my lifestyle, as close to paradise as you get. Posted up in a wonderful Starbucks.... oh and that brings up something I wanted to go over with the reader. You may have noticed I spend a lot of time posted up in Starbucks during the stories told in my books. Well, this is true. But for all of 2014 and 2015, I survived entirely off a 0-day hack of Starbucks gift cards that I came across, that allowed the endless refill of cash onto the gift cards. So, fuck Starbucks.

At the same moment that I was smoking my second pipe of weed and enjoying a latte in the late morning sun, a young black man by the name of Michael Brown was a thousand miles away walking down his residential street in a little city called Ferguson in the State of Missouri. He was confronted walking down the middle of his own trafficless residential street by Darren Wilson, who was driving a marked SUV and was an officer in the Ferguson Police Department. He was also white, and he didn't like Mike Brown. Not one bit. He slammed on his brakes approximately seventy-five feet from where Michael and a companion were strolling down their own street on a lazy summer morning, and he began to yell and shout at Mike to get the fuck out of the street and walk on the sidewalk.

What happened next takes a hundred times longer to tell than it did to happen. Michael Brown tossed Officer Darren Wilson the bird and just kept right on strolling home. Which is pretty much what any of us would have done, really. Darren Wilson flew into a rage, threw his vehicle into drive, and tore up next to Mike Brown - so close that when he threw open the door to his SUV to confront Mike, he slammed the door into Mike's shoulder....hard. Without thinking, Mike Brown spun around and slammed the door straight back shut, right in Darren Wilson's face - so hard he probably hurt him.

In a flash so fast it caught Mike totally by surprise, Darren Wilson drew his service weapon while still sitting in his cruiser, and pumped off two quick rounds, one of which missed and the other grazed Mike Brown in the shoulder. Mike managed to push Darren Wilson's wrist away, which is what prevented the second shot from taking his head off.

Then Mike Brown did the only sensible thing at that point. He ran....like hell. Officer Darren Wilson then exited his vehicle shouting and cussing and fired off another cluster of rounds at the back of a fleeing Michael Brown. At least two of the shots managed to strike Mike in the back. At this point, having been shot three times by an enraged Darren Wilson, Michael Brown knew he was finished no matter what. Standing now some 50 feet away from a steadily approaching Darren Wilson, Mike turned to face him, fell to his knees, and attempted to raise his hands in surrender. He was unable to fully lift one arm due to the injury to his shoulder.

Darren Wilson continued to stride towards a surrendering Mike Brown, calmly took aim, and proceeded to unload the rest of his clip into Michael Brown. He was nineteen, had just graduated high school, and was due to begin his first semester in college the following month. Now he was about to lay dead in the streets, bleed out in the blistering Missouri heat, in his own neighborhood for all to see, including his family who lived across the street - for four fucking hours.

As the entire community began to gather and make noise at the police tape surrounding Michael Brown's dead body, and the police responded to this modest gathering, not even a protest yet really, forty or so people, with five armoured vehicles and riot cops, and I ordered my second latte of the day, a locally popular rapper from St. Louis who went by the name Tef Poe - was making his way to the nearby city of Ferguson from his home in St. Louis.

When he got there, he took in the scene, snapped a picture of Michael Brown's dead body, covered, with a river of blood pouring out of him and down the street, and attached it to what I feel is one of the most historic tweets in history.

@TefPoe: We need international help, please! This is happening now!!

This is the moment where the magic of the Internet kicks in. I have no idea, I've never investigated, the exact chain of events that led to this young rapper's tweet to end up flashing down my Twitter time line, with its grizzly attachment, but it did. In seconds that plea for help flashed a thousand miles north and I saw it sitting in the Starbucks that sunny morning in Montreal. Now, I see a lot of grizzly pictures in my human rights work. So mind you there was nothing that initially caught my eye or made me pause. But as it scrolled by, it dawned on me, this wasn't the Middle East, this was from some bum-fuck city in Missouri called Ferguson! I paused over the picture. In retrospect, that was probably the exact moment that fate decreed the existence of *Anonymous Operation Ferguson.*

I flipped open a tab and attempted to chat with this Tef Poe, who was still there at the police tape tweeting in real-time about poor Michael Brown laying in the streets. I got through to him right away.

@CommanderXanon: Hello. I saw your message about wanting international help. You have perhaps heard of Anonymous?

@TefPoe: Everyone has heard of Anonymous!

@CommanderXanon: And you would be comfortable with a bunch of creepy hackers in Mask getting mixed up in this?

@TefPoe: Of course, absolutely. We have no one here. To be honest, this isn't really a protest, it's a grieving community. Yet they already have military grade force out. These people will go home and forget, it's all they can do, unless we get some help.

@CommanderXanon: Tell me why I should care. Not to be callous, but this shit goes down every day, and a lot of people need our help. What makes this kid, Mike Brown, any different?

There was a long pause, and I actually thought I had offended this rapper from St. Louis and this was where it was going to end. Then the reply came through.

@TefPoe: He was unarmed, on his knees, with his hands in the air, and the cop lit him up and emptied his clip into him.

He attached a picture that will live in infamy, of Michael Brown's step dad standing by the police tape in the immediate aftermath of the shooting, with the very first protest sign of what would become the *Ferguson Uprising*:

"The Ferguson Police Just Killed My Unarmed Son"

That's what was scrawled on a piece of torn cardboard with magic marker.

@CommanderXanon: Yeah....ok, I'm in. Let's do this. You'll need to have our back with a lot of Black folk, we are after all creepy hackers with Masks, they might not even know who we are at first. But I'll deliver the *Global Collective of Anonymous* to you by nightfall.

And from those humble beginnings the current iteration of *Black Lives Matter* and the Black Civil Rights movement in the USA began, on that fateful summer day back in August 2014 - with a conversation between a hacker and a rapper. And before they even came to collect Michael Brown's body from the street that afternoon, I had registered an *Anonymous Operation Ferguson* Twitter account, Top level Domain name, set up the website, and I was working on the Press Release and video with my *Crew* and a handful of *Anons* who learned I was launching something big and wanted in.

That night saw chaos in the streets of Ferguson the likes of which the USA has rarely witnessed. And the next thirty days would see some of the most frantic hacktivism of my career. Desperately multi-tasking that first night, I ran the Op Ferguson Twitter account to two effects, pushing out media reports from the ground, and pushing back to the activists on the ground good intelligence that could help them in the running street battles with the police. In addition, I rushed to finish the *Anonymous Operation Ferguson* official Press Release, while other *Anons* simultaneously worked to complete the accompanying video. When it was completed, I flipped open my Jabber with OTR and shot the PR and video to Gabriella Coleman for her take.

Anonymous Operation Ferguson - Press Release

Sunday - August 10, 2014 1:30 PM CST USA

A little over 24 hours ago in Ferguson, Missouri - USA the Ferguson Police Department shot an unarmed teen 6 times and killed him. His body was left to lie in a pool of blood in the sweltering heat for four hours while the police militarized the area against protesters and attempted to concoct a reasonable story as to why they snatched this innocent student's life for no reason.

The St. Louis County Sheriff Department even sealed the roads leading to Ferguson in a vain attempt to prevent protesters from reaching the city. His name was Mike Brown, he was 17 - and he would have started college next week. Instead, his family is struggling to come up with funeral costs.

The entire global collective of Anonymous is outraged at this cold-blooded murder of a young teen. Not a week goes by that some young person, usually of minority ethnicity - is slaughtered by murderous police in the USA. For this reason Anonymous will not be satisfied this time, as we have in the past - with simply obtaining justice for this young man and his family. Anonymous demands that the Congressional Representatives and Senators from Missouri introduce legislation entitled "Mike Brown's Law" that will set strict national standards for police conduct in the USA. We further demand that this new law include specific language to grant the victims of police violence the same rights and prerogatives that are already enjoyed nationwide by the victims of other violent criminals. The Equal Protection clause of the US Constitution demands nothing less.

To the good people of Ferguson, take heart - and take your streets. You are not alone, we will support you in every way possible. Occupy every square inch of your city. Open your homes and help in any way you can the protesters who will come to your city from every part of Missouri and the USA. Businesses and householders that are near protest rallies, open your WiFi routers so that live streamers and other independent journalists can use the Internet connections. Feed each other, keep each other safe - and stay in the streets until we are totally victorious in all our demands.

To the Ferguson Police Department and any other jurisdictions who are deployed to the protests: we are watching you very closely.

If you abuse, harass - or harm in any way the protesters in Ferguson we will take every web based asset of your departments and governments off line. That is not a threat, it is a promise. If you attack the protesters, we will attack every server and computer you have. We will dox and release the personal information on every single member of the Ferguson Police Department, as well as any other jurisdiction that participates in the abuse. We will seize all your databases and E-Mail spools and dump them on the Internet. This is your only warning.

The time has come for more than simple justice for these atrocities. The time has come to draw a line in the sand and say "no more dead kids", no more police killings and beatings. Anonymous is drawing a line in the sand, and that line runs right down the middle of Main Street Ferguson, Missouri. Police impunity ends with the barbaric death of Mike Brown.

We Are Anonymous - We Are Legion - We Will Not Forgive - We Will Not Forget

EXPECT JUSTICE - DEMAND CHANGE

------------------------------------------------------------------------

Web Site - www.OperationFerguson.cf

Twitter - twitter.com/OpFerguson2015

----------

biella: Wow.

Commander X: Someone just told me we may be starting the next civil rights movement in the USA tonight.

biella: I think they may be right!

Before midnight, the Anonymous Operation Ferguson Twitter account had eight thousand followers. And that's the true story of how the *Ferguson Uprising* began.

----------

Monday - August 10, 2014 approx. 7:00 AM ET - Starbucks Montreal, Quebec - CANADA

Day two of the *Ferguson Uprising* and *Anonymous Operation Ferguson* began with brush fires everywhere. Our Twitter, which had gained another two thousand followers while I slept a bit, topping out at over ten thousand followers - had been briefly suspended by Twitter. After reaching out to technical support, I got the first of many shocks in the weeks to come. The founder of Twitter, @jack, followed us and had intervened to restore and protect our account. Later that day he would fly to Ferguson, and over the next two days he marched in the streets and live tweeted like a pro. We could do no wrong from here on out, we were protected by the boss.

While I struggled to give a half dozen media interviews simultaneously, I was being introduced by Tef Poe to his room mate, Bassem Masri. Bassem Masri was a Palestinian. Which was an interesting coincidence, because the vast majority of the hackers who answered my original call to arms in Ferguson lived in Gaza. Bassem had tried his hand at livestreaming the previous night, and had taken a liking to it. Bassem was adamant that I understand one thing, that what I thought was a random and frantic attempt to push information back to and amongst the protesters had *worked* the night before.

As it turned out, the *Op Ferguson* Twitter account, which I only hoped may be mildly useful to the protesters on the ground in Ferguson, had in fact been indispensable. I spent several hours that morning working with Bassem to understand exactly how we were useful on social media to the protesters, and brainstorming ways that we could enhance that for tonight's action. Then the hacks began....

The first sign that a cyber strike was underway was the entire St. Louis County government cyber presence simply....disappeared. For several hours. Then a series of crippling E-Mail Bombs were detonated on their servers, as well as those belonging to the City of Ferguson, effectively shutting down E-Mail service countywide for five days. By that point there was really nothing left of either government entity, at least not on the Internet. They had been turned into smoking craters in cyber space. As these events were happening and being reported on in the media, something truly historic was unfolding in the streets of the tiny city of Ferguson. Tens of thousands of people were pouring into the streets, and being met by a truly dystopian vision. Huge armored vehicles with giant sniper rifles (manned) on top, and hundreds of fully armored and armed riot police. Since last night, the slogan "Hands Up, Don't Shoot" in honor of Michael Brown had been chanted. It was surreal to watch thousands of protesters, all with their hands in the air, facing off with what was essentially an occupying army of militarized "police".

As we all watched on the livestreams, the lines slowly formed up. There was a long moment of hushed silence as the protesters, hands in the air - stared sullenly at the snipers atop the armored vehicles, and the riot police lined up before them. Then one lady stepped forward with a bullhorn and what looked like it might be an actual soap box. She stood up on the box, and stopping to consult her mobile phone, she began to speak. She spoke about Michael Brown, and his family. She spoke about the police, just feet away. Then out of the blue, she addresses *Anonymous*.

So quickly I almost spilled my coffee, I flipped open the tab and tweeted back on the now iconic *Anonymous Operation Ferguson* Twitter account:

@OpFreguson2015: We can hear you! We are watching you now on the livestreams!

As I watched on the livestreams. the lady looked at her mobile, then looked up at the crowd and read out my tweet to them! I was a thousand miles away, and behind the *Mask of Anonymous*, and I was talking to these people via social media in real-time as they faced down the police! The lady raised her bullhorn, and asked the crowd: "do you love Anonymous?". They shouted affirmative in unison. "Then let's let them hear our gratitude!" and she began a chant of "We Love Anonymous". She consulted her phone again. My god, she was actually waiting for me to tweet at her again on the *Anonymous Operation Ferguson* account!

@OpFerguson2015: We love you too! We are so honored to stand with you, to stand for Mike Brown and with his family. We will never leave you!

There was a pause as everything streamed through buffers on the Internet, then the world and myself watched as the lady read my words on behalf of *Anonymous* to the people assembled. The people cheered. The cops looked more nervous than ever. It was a moment in cyber activism I will never forget.

----------

Monday - August 11, 2014 approx. 6:30 AM ET - Starbucks Montreal, Quebec - CANADA

Day three of the *Ferguson Revolution*. By now we had over fifteen thousand followers on Twitter, with no end in sight. I was feeling a bit like the original *Freedom Operations*, where I only got an hour or two of sleep a day for weeks on end. I would work all day, maybe 15 hours or so, until whatever coffee house I was in closed and threw me out. I would then sit down on the sidewalk and work another two and half hours off my battery power and their WiFi. After dark, it became a mad scramble to push out the protesters' reports and media links, and to push to them info useful in dealing with the fluid situation on the ground. I was literally tweeting so furiously I gave myself carpel tunnel syndrome, and my hands were almost paralyzed.

Days were spent dealing with a voracious media, networking with hackers from around the world, and giving organizing advice and knowledge to protesters on the ground. My day was to begin with a terribly important Skype call with a representative from *Anonymous Palestine*. He and his *Cell* had contacted me to ask if they could assist *Anonymous Operation Ferguson* and myself with some hacking skills. They were a very welcome addition to our growing cyber army. The Skype call was to brief him on the particulars of what we needed hacked, and the peculiar protocols of this particular Anonymous Operation. As we spoke, I could hear the muffled thud thud thud in the background, as the Israel Defense Forces once again pounded Gaza in a bombing campaign that was well under way at that time. Finally, I couldn't take it anymore.

Commander X: Look, brother - you don't have to do this for us, you should take care of your own situation there.

Anonymous Palestine: You mean the bombs? Don't worry, they're further away than they sound. Besides, we got this. And someday, we may need those people in Ferguson, and we know they'll be there for us.

*Anonymous Palestine* would go on to be our biggest asset in *Operation Ferguson*, and this isn't really surprising. If anyone knows what it is like to be targeted by racist security forces, it's the Palestinians. The hacks against the Missouri government and police networks began within the hour. Soon, there was not much left to mess with. And this very night, only three days in - and people were marching with Palestinian flags in the streets of the tiny city of Ferguson. And they were wearing *Guy Fawkes Masks*. By the end of the day, we had twenty thousand followers on our Twitter account, and counted the founder of Twitter and many other celebrities among them.

----------

Friday - August 15, 2014 approx. 6:30 AM ET - Second Cup Coffee House Montreal, Quebec - CANADA

Day ten of the *Ferguson Uprising*. We now had north of thirty thousand Twitter followers. People were on the ground in far more places than Missouri. Dozens of cities around the world began to stage sympathy protests with Ferguson. Millions were in the streets around the world. It was staggering and breathtaking, and *Anonymous* was right there from the first moment, doing our job and making a difference. My morning began pushing out a story of Tibetan Monks and Nuns who had flown in from Dharamsala, India to join in solidarity with those actually marching in the streets in Ferguson. Pictures of these wonderful Tibetan Buddhists across from the main protest encampment at the Ferguson Police Headquarters hugging what we had come to think of as "our" protesters, was something we worked hard to get to the media that day.

This is one role we always take on during the *Freedom Operations*, as anyone who read my first book surely knows.

**132**

We are the masters of media and propaganda, and we know it and wield it on behalf of ourselves and those we choose to stand up for. But in *Anonymous Operation Ferguson*, we augmented that with some very specific spin control aimed at the police and governments in Missouri, and their attempt to demonize the victim of this hot-blooded murder, and to make a saint out of the murderer. Our efforts at balancing the playing field in this regard was something that Michael Brown's mother would comment on when she secretly met with one of *Anonymous* representatives weeks later. She also decried the lack of more seriously transgressive hacking. Which I thought was especially humorous as we had been reported that day to have crossed the ten million in damages line and there was little left in Missouri to hack.

In the midday, I met online with Bassem Masri in an encrypted chat. He was a great and very funny guy. As I said previously, he was Tef Poe's roommate at the time, and in just ten brief days and with a huge help from *Anonymous*, we had managed to make him into a veritable global livestreaming star. I was liasoning with him now, because Tef Poe had become so saturated as the instigator of the entire thing that he was too overwhelmed to deal in fine-grained detail with his new "creepy hackers in masks" friends. (*Author's Note: That's a joke Tef*)

Bassem: This is such an honor Commander X. I want to thank you for everything you guys have done for us so far. I don't think we could have got this far without you guys.

X: Just X, the Commander nonsense is pretentious bullshit. This is just getting started, weve not even begun to fuck with them yet. That's what I wanted a meeting about. I wanted to see if I could use you, with Tef's backing, to be a pipeline to the protesters at the police station. Will you do that for us?

Bassem: of course, anything you want. Let me take notes hold on.

X: It's important that we open dialog with the protesters we're flying cover for. So I want the channel for general purposes going forward. But specifically tonight, they are having a big pow wow. Would like to send a specific and private message to them through you, if that's ok.

Bassem: Got my laptop open, shoot.

X: Tell them first, Anonymous loves them - as always. We will never leave you. And you are all doing wonderful, so brave, so courageous. But we'd like to encourage you to broaden your street tactics in the realm of the transgressive, just a little. Well, maybe a lot. Things that are often considered "old school" tactics, but they are still very effective, especially when you have the media's attention - as you all do globally at the moment. Here's a list of possibles, and you can innovate others:

1) Banner Drops

2) Gate/door lock downs

3) Freeway/train blockades

Stuff like this. I can send Bassem some PDF manuals on good practices for these tactics.

Bassem: Fuck X, that's damn good stuff. They are really going to appreciate this. I can't thank you enough.

X: No problem, I am here every minute of every day for you.

Later that night Bassem pinged me, it had been a long day - but it was worth talking to him again.

Bassem: Sorry to bother you so late X. I gave them your message and the docs X. They are going to start with some stuff tomorrow. They were blown away, and they wanted to send a message back to you, from the organizers, to Anonymous:

A Message From The Ferguson Protesters To Anonymous

We just wanted to say thank you to all you Anons that helped in Ferguson. We really couldn't have done this without you honestly. Thank you for protecting the protesters, and for thinking up the legislation that we're pushing for. You gave us a voice that no one can take away. I honestly appreciate you guys, I may not know you, and you probably don't know me, but I thank you from the bottom of my heart.

Today the protest was beyond awesome, the highway patrol captain even led it, and there were no problems. If it weren't for you guys, the police probably would have gassed the protesters again tonight, but because of y'all they didn't. The county cops were nowhere to be found, only highway patrol and city cops, who are pretty cool. On top of getting our voices out there in Ferguson, you have all helped to spread the word to where this is an International protest now. We have so much support, and we know that we aren't alone because of you guys. Thank you for giving us our voices back, and thank you for supporting us and helping us. You guys are honestly, amazing, even if I don't know who you are. I hope that you continue to help and support us until the legislation giving cops a strict protocol to follow when dealing with situations and the treatment has passed.

Thank you for giving us the start of our revolution and making it known that we can and will make a difference.

SINCERELY -- *The Ferguson Protesters*

This sort of shit happens to us in *Anonymous* all the time. But I have to tell you, it absolutely never grows old.

----------

Monday - August 18, 2014 approx. 8:30 AM ET   - Starbucks Montreal, Quebec - CANADA

Two weeks into the *Ferguson Uprising*. Today, I turned fifty years old. Half a century. A landmark most men celebrate with some amount of gusto. I actually forgot until almost noon, I was so busy with *Anonymous Operation Ferguson*. My gift to myself, this is no boast, to sleep exactly one hour extra in celebration. That is literally it. My barristas at my favorite coffee house made a hideous scene of bringing me a burning cupcake and singing horrendously out of tune, but it was thankfully over fast. Hundreds of cities and literally tens of millions were now marching every day for Ferguson and Michael Brown. The people most closely involved with *Anonymous Operation Ferguson* had met the night before, and we had decided to take it to the next level, by calling not only for passage of *Mike Brown's Law*, but the removal of the Governor of Missouri and later the Mayor of Ferguson. We were going for blood, and I spent the morning pushing out the Communique that was drafted:

Anonymous Operation Ferguson - Communique

Monday - August 18, 2014  11:15 AM CST

Last night the global collective of Anonymous watched in horror along with the rest of the world as the security forces that have besieged the small city of Ferguson, Missouri launched a brutal paramilitary assault on the good people of that city, who stood their ground for the cause of freedom and justice for Mike Brown - murdered by the same police.

**136**

And if this wasn't bad enough, the Governor of Missouri - having already declared martial law the day before, today announced the deployment of National Guard troops to be used against the protesters in Ferguson. We will not allow this situation to stand.

Governor Nixon: you have exercised extra-constitutional powers to illegally declare martial law, you have presided over the mass violation of the civil rights of the people of Ferguson, you have turned the City of Ferguson into an open air prison, and you have committed crimes against humanity so severe that for the first time in history Amnesty International has deployed a human rights monitoring team to the USA. You have shown yourself to be a criminal and an enemy of your own people. You have behaved like a dictator in the mid-east, and now Anonymous shall treat you as one. You see we have experience dealing with dictators.

Governor Nixon you are now dismissed. You will tender your resignation with the Secretary of State immediately. We will now begin the process, with which we are very familiar - of shutting down your illegitimate and illegal government. We will terminate your electronic communications, leak and dump all your data. We will remove you from the Internet, and your own people with the help of sympathetic legislators will remove you from power.

Furthermore, we will hold accountable and gather evidence against any member of the security forces or military who have harassed, abused, detained - or in any way molested either the protesters or journalists in Ferguson. This specifically includes independent journalists. For your ongoing crimes against the protesters in Ferguson each and every member of the police forces and National Guard deployed deserve nothing short of being locked up in their own jails. We will hold you all to account in manner and at a time of our choosing. You should expect us.

We Are Anonymous - We Are Legion - We Do Not Forgive - We Do Not Forget - Expect Us

----------

The reaction from the international human rights group *Amnesty* came fast. We had personally challenged them on Twitter with the Communique, and they responded by a first in US history. They sent a full human rights monitoring team to Ferguson the very day of the release. That night, they were promptly rounded up at shotgun point and escorted from the protest by Missouri State Police. Because they don't need no stinkin' human rights in their State. But at the protesters behest *Anonymous* had put out a worldwide call to action for everyone to make there way to Ferguson, or else march in their own streets no matter where they were. And it had worked. Scenes of white Black Bloc Street Medics carrying wounded black Ferguson teens from the field of battle were commonplace. Anarchists from California came by the bus load and found common cause and lived in harmony among the black run protest camps across the country and in Ferguson.

Anons went to the streets as they did during *Occupy OWS* and *Chanology*, showing up in Ferguson and handing out a thousand Guy Fawkes Masks to the locals the first night they arrived. And across the globe, hackers and information activists were turning their attention to basically any target we pointed them to. All we had to do is Tweet out on the *Anonymous Operation Ferguson* Twitter account that we weren't liking this website or we were wanting this cop's dox - and within hours at most it would appear as if by magic. And today we crossed the thirty-thousand follower threshold on our Twitter account. astounding given that I created it a little over two weeks prior, literally as Mike's body still lay in the streets.

----------

Thursday - October 23, 2014 approx. 4:30 PM ET - McGill University Montreal, Quebec - CANADA

I did take several days off from working on *Anonymous Operation Ferguson* to have a little adventure when one *Glenn Greenwald* decided to come calling in our beautiful city of Montreal. I first found out Glenn Greenwald was doing a speaking engagement in Montreal from the Twitter account of Gabriella Coleman. I immediately did two things. First, I messaged an Anon who lives in Quebec – and told them to prepare to come down for the event. The next thing I did was to write an E-Mail to Glenn offering to make myself available to him while he was in Montreal. To my huge surprise, I received an answer back almost immediately. Glenn not only wanted to meet with me in private, but was apparently quite anxious to do so. After bouncing a few messages with Glenn's "secretary" we settled on a meeting in the lobby of Glenn's hotel this evening before his speaking event at McGill University. At that point, I honestly thought it would just be an interesting evening – maybe some drinks after. Little did I know Glenn Greenwald's visit would precipitate quite a little three day adventure for us *Anons* here in Canada.

On the afternoon prior to the speaking event, the *Anon* from Quebec City arrived at the coffee house we were meeting at. This person was very excited to not only meet Glenn Greenwald, but later Gabriella Coleman. "Biella" as she is affectionately known within *Anonymous* was hosting Glenn's talk and she had agreed to meet with us both prior to the event at her office on McGill University campus. Surprisingly, there was no real "cloak & dagger" type preparations for the meeting with Glenn. Our plan was to show up in the lobby of his hotel and have the front desk call him.

When we arrived in the lobby of the hotel however, I began to sweat – and it wasn't because of the heat. As it really began to sink in exactly who I was about to meet with, (not to mention who was doing the meeting) –

I noticed what seemed like an inordinate number of individuals around us wearing suits and ties. Granted, it was a high-end business hotel – but there still seemed like a lot of suits were about. How many of them were foreign intelligence agents? CIA? What seemed like a straight forward meeting with yet another journalist was now starting to feel a bit more…dangerous. It got really weird when the desk lady called Glenn and suddenly turned to me and asked "who's calling?". Me and the other *Anon* briefly looked at each other and then I turned back, coughed once and said "tell him it's *X*". I'll give the girl credit for being a pro, she only hesitated about a half a second before complying.

The other *Anon* and myself then found a comfortable looking area in the sprawling lobby out of the way (and as far away from the "suits" as we could get), and settled in to await one of the most famous journalists in modern times. A few minutes later Glenn Greenwald bounded down the steps and looked us over. I stood up and straightened out the "Guy Fawkes" hoodie I was wearing and smiled at him. He strode right up to me and shook my hand with a firm grasp and said "X, I presume?". I introduced my companion and then we all settled in to our corner of the lobby.

Over the course of the next couple of hours I had one of the most fascinating and stimulating conversations I have ever had with a journalist. Normally when I am meeting a journalist, even one as esteemed as say the editor of *Rolling Stone* – I am still the most famous person in the equation. But to sit there in that lobby talking information activism with the journalist who published the Snowden leaks, the single most trusted and hated journalist in the western world – was an incredibly unique experience.

There were some secrets shared. But much of what we discussed was about information activism, and the various factions within this movement and how those factions relate to each other. So for example, I filled Glenn in on the details of the great "Paywall Battle" between *Anonymous* and *WikiLeaks* that erupted in 2012.

We discussed the relationship and differences between hacktivists and whistle blowers. And we discussed my own self-imposed political exile in Canada and it's implications, for myself and for the movement. We talked a lot about *Anonymous* and it's critical role in the information activism, past Ops and future possibilities.

One thing I want to portray about Glenn Greenwald is his personality did not conform to what I had been led to expect. He was not in any way aloof or high on himself. Despite being clearly exhausted he bounded across the lobby, shook my hand with great enthusiasm – and was lively, curious – and engaged throughout our wide-ranging conversation. He was genuinely pleasant, down to earth – and wanting to know anything we could tell him about Anonymous. We spent a lot of time discussing the sacrifice of not only the whistleblowers like Snowden, but the hackers like Jeremy Hammond and journalists like Barrett Brown. Glenn was particularly curious (and genuinely concerned) about how I was holding up under the rigors of nearly 3 years in exile and hiding.

This evening my companion and I made our way onto McGill University and began the almost comical adventure of trying to locate the tiny and disorganized office of one *Gabriella Coleman* – the famous anthropologist who studies hackers. We were going to the meeting ostensibly to score signed copies of her new book *Hacker, Hoaxer, Whistleblower, Spy*, but we were both hopeful of spending some quality time with *Biella* – who is so beloved within *Anonymous*. After many wrong turns, we finally stumbled upon Coleman's "office". Apparently holding the *Wolfe Chair* at McGill does not entitle one to an office with a bathroom. Biella's office was small, cramped, disorganized (but not untidy) and yes, right in plain sight as we walked in there was a Guy Fawkes mask resting lazily on a shelf.

Gabriella Coleman's research assistant Matt was there. And just prior to our arrival Biella had received a rather disturbing phone call from the Campus Security Office.

Apparently a viable death threat against Glenn Greenwald had been made, and the security for that night's event was being tightened. Glenn was not even going to be allowed to walk the short distance across the quad to the lecture hall, but was to be driven instead. However, with the weirdness and the book signing thing out of the way – we settled in to enjoy a delightful meeting with Gabriella Coleman. We touched on everything from Anonymous Operation Ferguson to how pissed off Barrett Brown was about some of the stuff in Biella's new book. Coleman and her research assistant were particularly curious about a controversy called "gamer-gate" and our thoughts on it.

Finally the time arrived for my companion and I to make our way to the venue for that night's event. We scored some excellent seats up front near the VIP section and waited for Biella to take the stage and introduce the star of the evening, Glenn Greenwald. I won't waste time trying to summarize Glenn's talk that night because you really should simply watch it for yourself below...

http://media.mcgill.ca/en/content/glenn-greenwald-conference-video-online

Glenn Greenwald's presentation was consummate, being directly applicable in every way to the Canadian audience in attendance. He was able to use his time on stage to brilliantly lead his audience through the Snowden and other leaks, their highlights – and why these disclosures are important to Canadians. When he was finished he took many questions from eager students in the audience.

After the event, my *Anon* companion and myself were due to meet Gabriella Coleman and some other friends for drinks. But we had an hour or so to kill so we headed to a local sandwich shop to grab a bite to eat.

Despite the fact that we were only inside for about 30 minutes, someone broke into my friends car and stole his laptop and both signed copies of *Hacker, Hoaxer, Whistleblower, Spy*. Were we the victims of some cagey intelligence people following Glenn and trying to see if we passed him anything? Or was it just an incredible coincidence and really bad luck? We'll never know I guess.

Anonymous and the information activist community are a tight-knit group, like family really. Later that night as we all gathered at a couple of different watering holes to celebrate Glenn's visit – there was much consternation at the theft of my friends laptop (the signed books were happily replaced the next day by Biella, who joked on Twitter she hoped the thieves would at least read it!). By the end of the evening a secret collection had raised more than enough to replace the computer stolen from my friends car. And just to add a touch of Black Hat to the evening, on the way home late that night we made a brief stop to pick up a package at a friends house. His doorbell didn't work, and we only had Skype on mobile so we needed WiFi to call upstairs to get his attention. Undeterred, I went back to the car and grabbed my laptop – sat down on the sidewalk in front of my buddies house – and calmly hacked his WiFi password so we could call him....

All in a nights work, really.

----------

Saturday - October 31, 2014 approx. 6:00 AM ET  - Starbucks Montreal, Quebec - CANADA

As I will detail later in this Chapter, *Anonymous Operation Ferguson* ended up being so huge, that it spawned an entire galaxy of baby or satellite Ops. One of those was the infamous war between *Anonymous* and the *Ku Klux Klan*. Today was the day this incredible, epic, and historic confrontation began, with the following official *Anonymous* Press Release:

**143**

Greetings Citizens of the World --

We are Anonymous.

When people are faced with grave injustices, those cries do not go unheard. We know who you are. We know the dangerous extent to which you will go to cover your asses. Originally, we did not attack you for your beliefs as we fight for freedom of speech. We attacked you due to your threats to use lethal force in the Ferguson protests. We took this grudge between us rather seriously. You continue to threaten anons and others. We never said we would only strike once.

The anons involved in this operation still believe you no longer particularly deserve the right to Freedom of Speech and Freedom to Assemble but that is not up to us. Let us make this especially clear: We are not oppressing you, Ku Klux Klan. We are not here to strip you of your Freedom of Speech. Anonymous will never strip you of any of your Constitutional rights. There is no "hate speech" exception to the Constitution. In a free society, we do have a duty to protect free thought, even when especially offensive. Your hateful ideas and words remain yours to keep. You are allowed to speak and in kind, we are allowed to respond. You are legally free to live and be any which way you choose to live and be. Keep in mind, it is not illegal nor oppressive to hurt your feelings. With that said – We are stripping you of your anonymity. Again. This is our protected speech.

After closely observing so many of you for so very long, we feel confident that applying transparency to your organizational cells is the right, just, appropriate and only course of action. You are abhorrent. Criminal. You are more than extremists. You are more than a hate group. You operate much more like terrorists and you should be recognized as such. You are terrorists that hide your identities beneath sheets and infiltrate society on every level.

The privacy of the Ku Klux Klan no longer exists in cyberspace. You've had blood on your hands for nearly 200 years. You continue to inflict civil rights violations, commit violent crimes and solicit others to commit violent criminal acts. You seek to intimidate and/or eliminate those that are different from you and those that you dislike by any means possible. You seek to terrorize anyone and anything that you feel is a threat to your narrow view of the "American way of life".

The last time we took your hoods off, you claimed to be misunderstood. Victimized. No. You are a damaged, dangerous, fragmented, splintered and amorphous collection of terroristic cells with a hate-based ideology and a well-documented history of violence against the American public – assault, murder, terrorism. You play a deep, damaging and historically sinister and malevolent role in the United States. We understand you far too well. You made a clear and ever present enemy of Anonymous when you threatened the lives of protesters and the men and women representing Anonymous on the ground in Ferguson, Missouri in November of 2014. You continue to make threats to anons you believe you have identified, journalists, anyone in the public that speaks out against your behavior. Your threats and intimidation are unprovoked, unwanted and will not be tolerated. Enough is enough.

Anonymous that we awakened a sleeping giant within you. We are here to remind you once again – you summoned an unslayable dragon. Anonymous is an idea. This fight will go on as long as it has to. The aim of this operation is digital. Another cyber war trist, nothing more. We are not violent. We will release, to the global public, the identities of up to 1000 klan members, Ghoul Squad affiliates and other close associates of various factions of the Ku Klux Klan across the Unites States.

To the government representing the people of the United States of America:

The American public should not be subjected to victimization by hate groups through a hate group's protection by the United States Constitution without additional laws in place to protect potential victims of these violent organizations. More dialogue is needed to create working solutions.

To the Citizens of the World:

We stand with you always, against oppression and injustice. Anonymous is many things. The anons participating in Operation KKK believe that it is a civic responsibility to be conscious and self-critical of our society in order to improve upon the shape of things to come.

To those that really disagree with us:

Sorry for the inconvenience, but not really. We are trying to change our world.

To the freedom fighters representing Anonymous in Ferguson, Missouri:

Stay the course.

*how you can help*

You can show your support for us lawfully by raising awareness of this operation through sharing your thoughts and ideas about the KKK through tweetstorms and other social media amplication strategies. The ability to share information quickly and effectively will carry this operation far and wide.

146

Tag #OpKKK #HoodsOff when you post on social media platforms.

----------

Using *LocalLeaks*, we had begun to vacuum up all the *dox's* that the *Anonymous Operation KKK* folks were beginning to dump in massive troves. We ended uploading it all to the famous *Ferguson Files* section we set up when we engaged and weaponized *LocalLeaks* to use in Ferguson, just as we so successfully deployed it in Steubenville. We called the sub-section, obviously - *The KKK Files*. Later everything we collected was collated, and compressed into a download zip file. That file was transmitted to various hate group monitoring orginizations with which *Anonymous* had formed a relationship of trust. *Anonymous Operation KKK* persists to the release of this book, and has become much more active since the unfortunate election of *Donald Trump* as President of the USA and the commensurate rise in hate crimes and prominence of various hate groups and their members. It remains the most outstanding example of the baby or satellite Ops that were beginning to spin in the orbit of *Anonymous Operation Ferguson*.

----------

Wednesday - November 5, 2014 approx. 6:30 AM ET - Second Cup Coffee House  Montreal, Quebec - CANADA

Three months. That's how long the *Ferguson Uprising* and *Anonymous Operation Ferguson* had been going. I had never in my entire career in *Anonymous* logged this amount of time in any Operation. Working every day with Anons and Information Activists all over the world, and even a small cadre here in Montreal, I usually put in twelve to fifteen hours a day. But today was special.

**147**

One of the amazing things to develope in *Anonymous Operation Ferguson* was a tiny *Anonymous* Cell called simply *Anonymous Ferguson*. A decent number of mostly young *Ferguson Protesters* had full on adopted the identity of *Anonymous*, and regularly appeared together as a group at Ferguson protests wearing very nicely customized *Guy Fawkes Masks*. They became famous for the creation of the infamous "Mike Brown" car, a raucously decorated and stickered protest vehicle that frankly it was a good thing it didn't have to leave the city, it seemed in that bad a repair. But with ten Masked *Anons* in and on top of it, wearing *Mask* and carrying *Anonymous* and upside down American flags, it was a sight to behold indeed.

I had kept in daily touch with this wonderful *Crew*, and we had cooked up something super special for Ferguson tonight. Because today was the fifth of November, an iconic day for *Anons* all over the world. The day we all go to the streets in hundreds of cities around the world, by the millions, wearing *Masks*, and do our annual *Anonymous Million Mask March* event.

*"Remember, remember - the fifth of November and the Gunpowder Treason and plot. I know no reason why the Gunpowder treason should ever be forgot."*

And this year a new city would join the list of those holding a MMM. The tiny City of Ferguson Missouri was about to celebrate *Guy Fawkes Day* in style, and stage their very own *Million Mask March*. Our little *Anon Crew* on the ground was excited as could be. Bassem Masri had graciously helped a great deal in organizing the event, creating a general set of actual activities with my assistance and advice. He had also provided the critical component of a few bullhorns and batteries, and finally trusty as ever, Bassem would help us capture and stream the event from Ferguson to the world. The legendary *Tef Poe* had agreed to make an appearance, and at Bassem's urging, even he was going to wear a Guy Fawkes Mask for the night. Tonight, everyone was an *Anon*.

**148**

It was, frankly, fucking heart-breakingly beautiful.

A little after dark, with about three hundred people gathered, Bassem found some sort of box and jumped up on it, lifted his Mask (to a huge cheer, he is beloved in Ferguson) and got everyone's attention with the bullhorn. A hush descended on the crowd of Masked Ferguson protesters, they had been primed on social media all day for the starting ceremonies. They were especially keen to hear the words that they had been promised had been transmitted to them from *Anonymous Operation Ferguson* and the *Global Collective*. Words that they would hear shortly, because I had written them myself just hours before.

Bassem Masri: Ok, hey yo - listen up y'all. Anonymous has been here from day one. They have had our backs every single day. Today, they are all watching us. So this protest, this Million Mask March, this is for all our new *Anon* brothers and sisters all over the world. This is our thank you. We are one of you now.

So, yo so listen....*Anonymous Operation Ferguson*, anyone here heard of them?

(the crowd cheers)

Yeah me too. Anyway they sent us a message. I have an *Anon* here from Ferguson, she's going to read it to you so pay attention, alright!

By now there were tens of thousands of Anons around the world, some still marching in the streets of their own cities, who were tuned into Bassem Masri's livestream that night. And his was one of three good ones. I had never heard it that quiet in the street across from Ferguson PD during these protests.

As a line of riot cops protecting Ferguson PD headquarters shuffled in silence and leaned on their shields, a tiny young black women we knew online as "AnonLine" stepped up on the little platform, lifted up her colourful Guy Fawkes Mask just enough to speak into it, took up the bullhorn, and stared intently at the piece of paper Bassem held up for her. All you could hear was the cameras of dozens of media people clicking. The whole world was quite literally watching this young black woman, and I began to shake uncontrollably as I watched the livestream. She coughed once, quietly - and spoke softly yet firmly into the bullhorn. In the silence, her voice sounded like it could be heard in Saint Louis. She read slowly, clearly, and with great deliberation. She never faltered. She was flawless.

Hello everyone. I'm a little nervous, so please be patient with me. This is: A Message from *Anonymous Operation Ferguson* to the 2014 Million Mask March here in Ferguson:

Greetings everyone!  We want you to know we are with you, we can see you all at this very moment on the live streams and we are listening as our sister Anon reads our words to you. We LOVE you!! You all look AWESOME!!

Welcome, Ferguson - to your first ever Million Mask March!  You are now part of a noble tradition. All around the world today millions of your fellow Anons have peacefully marched on their seats of government and let their presence be known to those who walk the halls of power. From Washington DC to Cairo Egypt, from London to Manila - over 450 cities and upwards of 2 million people have participated in this year's *Anonymous Million Mask March*. And this year is extra special, because so many of us Anons around the world have worked so very hard on *Anonymous Operation Ferguson*.

So many days you have brought tears to our eyes with your courage and fortitude, and today is one of those days. And to watch the live streams and see you all gathered like this, it makes us laugh, smile - and weep.

Anonymous is a part of this great *Ferguson Movement*. In the moments after Mike Brown was shot, local artist Tef Poe reached out on the Internet for help. His anguished cry was heard almost immediately by an *Anon*. Before Mike Brown's body was collected from the streets of Ferguson, we had registered the now iconic @OpFerguson2015 Twitter account. An hour later, we registered the Top level Domain for our website www.OperationFerguson.cf. Later that same night we sent out our first Tweets, and by the following morning we had over two thousand followers!  Now, over 33 thousand of you trust us and follow our Twitter account - where we do our best every day to network and share information with you; the protesters. We have been with you since before they washed Mike Brown's blood from the street, and we will *never* leave you. The entire *Global Collective of Anonymous* is with you constantly, working, watching - and helping in any way we can think of.

Now, some of our critics - both yours and ours, have tried to label us as "outside agitators", saying that we sit safely behind our keyboards while we let you the protesters take all the risks. Nothing could be further from the truth. First, *Anons* from all over the world have traveled to Ferguson and have been gassed, shot and arrested in your streets right along with you. And *Anons* will keep doing this. But even the *Anons* who have chosen to fight with you online face grave danger. We have all received, just as you have - hundreds of death threats. Some of them from law enforcement. And you should know that in every *Anonymous Operation* we have ever done in the USA, *Anons* have eventually been arrested for cyber protest.

And while it may only be a few that eventually face this persecution, due to the archaic Computer Fraud And Abuse Act they will face *decades* in prison for helping you online. But we are not afraid. It is our great honor and privilege to fight this epic battle with you. Today the greatest honorary *Anon* at this gathering is Mike Brown himself! Do not doubt for a moment he is here with us. And he is laughing his ass off at how silly we all look. We *will* get justice for our brother. We WILL get justice for ALL the victims of police brutality. And we *will* stop the killing.

Anonymous is a *Global* Collective. We recognize no borders or ethnic distinctions. We believe in one thing: FREEDOM. I want you all to know that *Anons* from over 75 countries have participated and will continue to participate in *Anonymous Operation Ferguson*. During that first fiery week, I recall being on a Skype call with our fantastic *Anons* in Gaza, Palestine. *Anonymous Palestine* had offered to assist us, and I was briefing them on some info. At the time, Israel was carpet bombing Gaza and killing hundreds of civilians with indiscriminate shelling. I could actually hear the dull thuds of the bombs falling around my friend over the Skype. I was like fuck brother, you don't have to do this you know - if you have something else you need to be doing for your people. He smiled and said no way, it's all good. Besides he said, someday we will need those people in Ferguson and they will be there for us!

Today you make your entrance into the *Global Collective of Anonymous*. And for the foreseeable future, you will receive the attention and aid of this worldwide family. But this is a *privilege*, and one that comes with *responsibilities*. Someday, when we have won justice and brought an end to the killing - it will be *your* turn to give back to the *Global Collective*. It will be *your* turn to roll up your sleeves, don your *Masks* - and help others around the world who are desperately fighting the oppressors for their freedom.

And we have no doubt you will do so admirably. For you are not just any *Anons*. Like our comrades in Egypt, Tunisia, Turkey and Greece - you are *Anons* born from the *fires of revolution*. You are *Anons* created in the *crucible of street battles* with merciless security forces. You will fight well, and *Anonymous* is immensely stronger for having you in our *Global Collective*.

(at this point the poor girl had to stop as the crowd broke into a roar and a chant of "we are legion, we are anonymous")

Many of you have written and said that *we* are *your* heroes. But on this day Ferguson we want you to know something: you are some of the most brilliant, creative, beautiful and *courageous* people we have ever had the honor of fighting with. You honor us by allowing us the *privilege* to stand with you. And never forget this: YOU ARE OUR HEROES!!

Now, we are going to end this message in the usual way. But we want to ask you to do something. As our Anon reads each line we would like you to repeat it back to her, as LOUD as you possibly can. Let your voices be heard by those in power, and let them tremble in dread at the justice that is coming!

WE ARE ANONYMOUS

WE ARE LEGION

WE ARE EVERYWHERE

WE ARE FERGUSON

WE DO NOT FORGIVE MURDER

**153**

WE WILL NOT FORGET MIKE BROWN

EXPECT US

At that point as they say, the crowd went wild. And the police line took two steps....backward. All I could do was bury my face in my arms and weep uncontrollably. It was just that type of Op. I would never be the same again, these people were going to change me forever. Their pain and hurt would be seared into my soul by sharing their anguish in such a prolonged and personal fashion. But let me fucking tell all of you reading this book something right now. That young woman is *Anonymous*. And what she did that night, bravely reading out the words I had written on behalf of the *Global Collective* I love so much, that is the whole point of all of this. At moments like these my own plight and sacrifices, considerable though they are, for the cause of *Anonymous* - they are all paid for in full each time. *This is why I do it.*

----------

Wednesday - November 24, 2014 approx. 6:30 PM ET - Second Cup Coffee House  Montreal, Quebec - CANADA

The *Ferguson Uprising* had been in full swing daily for over three and a half months now. While Michael Brown's family was set to get a quiet financial settlement from the City of Ferguson, which was essentially war weary from three and a half months of daily raucous protests, this "blood money" in no way was the measure of justice that *Anonymous* had in mind when it joined me and Tef Poe that fateful day and stood up for Michael Brown - even as he lay dead in the streets on August 9th. No. What we had in mind resembled more of a *murderous cops behind bars* flavor of justice. And thus, for us, and most of the protesters, who agreed with us - it had all come down to tonight.

**154**

Unfortunately *Anonymous Operation Ferguson, LocalLeaks* and I - had ruined the surprise for the world and the protesters. The government had tried to hush up everything, but we leaked it all several weeks prior, on October 27th to be exact, when we published the *Grand Jury Leaks* section of the *Ferguson Files*:

On October 27, 2014 *Anonymous Operation Ferguson* released a disclosure based upon a series of leaks from two sources. Having decided that LocalLeaks was better positioned to handle the material already leaked to them, as well as all Ferguson related leaks going forward - Anonymous turned over all leaked material, both published and unpublished - to LocalLeaks for analysis and publication.

Below is the full text from the original Grand Jury/Darren Wilson disclosure published by Anonymous Operation Ferguson on October 27, 2014 at 3:00 PM ET USA. In this disclosure Anonymous reveals that the Grand Jury decision will be officially released by authorities in St. Louis on or about November 10, 2014 and that the decision will be to NOT indict Ferguson Police Officer Darren Wilson for the murder of the un-armed teen Mike Brown. The disclosure further reveals that Darren Wilson will not face any judicial process at the federal level either. And finally the disclosure reveals some interesting details about the current situation of Officer Darren Wilson, who remains a Ferguson Police Officer on paid leave. The original pastebin disclosure is below.

http://pastebin.com/CJ5ipU7W

Last night we announced that we have received over the past several days a series of leaks from two separate and unrelated sources regarding the long awaited Grand Jury decision regarding the murder of Mike Brown by Ferguson PD Officer Darren Wilson.

In our opinion after careful analysis the sources are reliable, and the information we are about to reveal is true. Both sources are government employees with access to both internal government as well as confidential police communications. For reasons of safety we will not be revealing anything further on either our sources or the material leaked to us. The following is a synopsis of the leaked information:

On or about November 10, 2014 the Grand Jury decision will be announced. Darren Wilson will NOT be indicted on ANY charges related to the murder of Mike Brown. All local police Chiefs and jail commanders have been notified to begin preparing for major civil unrest. Governor Nixon has been notified of the impending announcement and has ordered the Missouri National Guard to begin preparations for a possible re-enstatement of the martial law that was declared at the beginning of the Ferguson protests.

As additional evidence that neither the State nor Federal authorities intend any legal action against Darren Wilson for the murder of Mike Brown, one of our sources has provided a very intriguing close up glimpse of Darren Wilson - his current whereabouts and lifestyle. Darren Wilson is still in the St. Louis area and recently attended a Blues game. He has been made aware of the impending Grand Jury and US DOJ decisions in his favor and is now comfortable enough that he has just closed purchase on a new home in the south county area. He is still cohabitating with his girlfriend Officer Barbara Spradling of the St. Louis Police Department, who is now pregnant with their first child.

I guess his paid vacation for murder has been productive in more ways than one. In an attempt to "protect" himself, Darren Wilson has altered his appearance. His hairline & hair color have been altered and he has grown a substantial beard.

He is operating under the alias "Darren Obrien" or another false identity. (LocalLeaks note: On November 9, 2014 we received a credible leak indicating that in anticipation of the Ferguson Grand Jury announcement Officer Darren Wilson has been moved to a St. Louis County Police safe house in Oakville, MO.)

Finally on an unrelated note. "Josie" who called into a radio station during the early days of the Ferguson protests and purported to give Darren Wilson's "side" of the story, from which many conservative media outlets (such as FOX News) have since spun the most outlandish falsehoods - has been identified as an account assistant at Javelin, Inc. and is associated with the Ferguson PD. We are still gathering info on this person and what exactly her relationship is with the FPD and her interest in Mike Brown's murder. (LocalLeaks note: we have received info that "Josie" has deleted her facebook and other social media since the publication of this disclosure. We have received more information on this individual and will be posting it at a later date)

-- Secret ADM Global Intelligence Report --

On November 7, 2014 as a massive military and police build up began in Ferguson and St. Louis, involving everything from dozens of armored personnel carriers, hundreds of police officers (some from as far away as Detroit) and even military attack helicopters - LocalLeaks received a startling document. The document leaked to us is a secret intelligence report prepared by the private intelligence provider Global Security exclusively for the international corporation Archer Daniels Midland. Due to the desperate need of the people of Ferguson and St. Louis for information, we immediately released a photograph of the document on our Twitter account. The most pertinent thing revealed, and what the people of Missouri and the USA most wanted to know - is the exact date and time of the Grand Jury decision announcement.

We now know, thanks to this disclosure - that the announcement will come on November 10, 2014 (just as Anonymous had disclosed earlier) at or after 2:00 PM CT USA. Several confidential sources have informed us that employees of Archer Daniels Midland have been quietly told to not report to work on Tuesday and Wednesday (November 11 & 12, 2014), lending further credence to the date/time of the Grand Jury announcement revealed in this disclosure. (LocalLeaks note: The day after we publicly released this document, the County Prosecutor's Office issued a statement that the announcement of the Grand Jury decision would probably come on or around November 15, 2014. We believe this change in plans was a direct result of our disclosure, in fact we anticipated just such an action by authorities while preparing the release. We also believe this change in release date reflects a desperate attempt by authorities to confuse the protesters in Ferguson and keep them off balance.)

While the most important revelation at the moment this document was disclosed by us was the all important time/date of the Grand Jury announcement, this document, which appears to be extremely informed and well sourced - contains a number of very disturbing revelations regarding an attempt by local police agencies to engage in extremely dangerous fear mongering and the propagation of panic. One of the most glaring examples is the police claiming that Islamic extremists may attempt to use the pandemonium of the protests to launch terror attacks in the local area. Another example is the police claiming that criminal gangs would use the cover of the protests to perpetrate crime sprees, and yet another is the claim that rival gangs would use the protests as cover to "settle scores". (LocalLeaks note: we have solid intelligence from the STL area that local "gangs" have in fact set aside their differences and united to join and defend the protests)

All in all, this disturbing document represents local police agencies targeting the local citizens as though they were enemies of the state, and preparing a full-blown military and war-like response to their free speech activities. This sort of overt and covert militarization can not but escalate tensions and create a climate of fear and distrust that will inevitably lead to violence. It would almost seem to be the intent of the police agencies involved to foment this violence. On November 13, 2014 the Missouri Ku Klux Klan publicized a flyer that they had been handing out in several St. Louis area neighborhoods in which they promised to attend in force any protests that developed as a result of the Ferguson Grand Jury announcement. In the release, they threatened to use lethal force against protesters, whom they termed "terrorists". In an interview given to MSM later that day by a leader of the Missouri KKK, the claim was made that the KKK had consulted with the Ferguson and St. Louis Police Departments and that they planned to work in concert. This claim was not refuted or denied by either Department. On a side note, the Global Collective of Anonymous sprang into action almost immediately and took down all the KKK websites in Missouri. On the following day, Anonymous released the names, photos and personal information on dozens KKK members in Missouri.

----------

So, that was it - the beans were spilled. And tonight's official announcement ritual was a cruel farce. The mood amongst the tens of thousands of protesters who had gathered in the streets of Ferguson, and the hundreds of thousands marching in solidarity in cities all over the world, was grim indeed. The small city had been overrun by tens of thousands of National Guard and police personnel from every jurisdiction within a thousand miles of Ferguson. Their mood was equally grim.

Everyone knew what would happen next, and there was absolutely nothing anyone could do to stop it. Ferguson, and swaths of other American cities, were about to burn. It's at moments like these that the gritty reality of slogans like *No Justice, No Peace* become clear.

The idiots in the government had for some unfathomably stupid reason scheduled the announcement for an hour after dark. There were sullen conversations, and weak attempts at chants, from the gigantic crowd that was still growing by the minute in front of the Ferguson Police Headquarters building. Armored personnel carriers with National Guard snipers on the roofs growled around the edges of the crowd. In all my years of protest, I had never seen anything like this. The tension was palpable, you could cut it with a knife. I actually became sick, nauseous, from the stress. So much work, and it looked like it was all about to go up in flames.

In the center of the crowd, where the police held the least sway - the protesters began to erect a small stage and modest sound system. As the government officials took their places in the press conference inside, Michael Brown's entire family took the stage in the center of this huge crowd arc-lit by hundreds of media trucks and cameras. Mike's mother was more grim than I had ever seen her, even at his funeral months before. She looked exhausted, and I had no doubt that our recent disclosure on *LocalLeaks* had done its part in making her lose sleep the past couple of weeks. I wept....

I flashed upon the meeting our *Crew* member had with Michael Brown's mother some weeks prior. *Anonymous* had already established informal and back-channel communications with representatives of Michael Brown's family - but this was the first time we had an *Anon* meet directly with them. I was live streamed the meeting on a private back channel. His mom stood for private as yet unpublished pictures with our Masked *Crew* member. And she thanked us profusely, and told us all the members of the family with the exception of Mike's Grandmother supported our involvement in her son's case. I continued to weep uncontrollably....

Of course, Darren Wilson would face no justice for the murder of Michael Brown. They announced no indictment. But Mike Brown's stepfather, whose iconic picture of himself as the very first Ferguson Protester had started this all on August 9th, pushed himself onto the stage and grabbed the microphone. The silence was deafening. And then he tilted his head back and roared. He began to rant, to scream and shout....and he told them to burn everything. I shit you not. Twenty-thousand people, in rapt attention to the stage, and he told them to burn it all. Michael's mother never even got a chance to speak. No one did. As Michael's father wrestled a still screaming stepfather off the little stage, other young men in the Brown entourage hustled Mike's mom to safety. Within seconds, all hell broke loose. The stupid government spokesperson or whoever was still calmly going on on television about how we all needed to respect the justice system, when the first volley of flash bang grenades and tear gas were launched from the police/Guard lines. It all happened so fast that....I don't know, even three seconds seems generous really.

Fuck me! I went into emergency overdrive. I had worked out certain "riot protocols" with Bassem and Tef Poe the night before, and I wasted no time firing off all emergency measures with a purpose. The rest of the night is a blur of trying to find out if my friends were still alive, and trying to aid the insurgents against the security forces any way we could. *Anonymous Operation Ferguson* had now finished its slow transition from a *Justice Operation* to a *Freedom Operation*. I never stopped weeping. Not for hours.

----------

Sunday - August 9, 2015 approx. 12:30 PM ET - Starbucks Toronto, Ontario - CANADA

What a difference a year can make. In your life. In your soul. In the history of movements.

In the history of the world. They say a single moment can change your life and world forever. Imagine a year filled with countless millions of those life changing moments, and you have *Anonymous Operation Ferguson*. None of us, and dozens were involved just at the very core - none of us in *Anonymous Operation Ferguson* got out unscathed. The death threats from law enforcement alone, one of the scariest parts, continue unabated to the release of this book.

I spent the sunny Sunday morning in Toronto quietly composing and sending messages to Bassem, Tef Poe, Michael Brown's mother, a few others. This was not the sort of anniversary you "celebrated". It was one of those you only hoped to endure with a little dignity and honor. I held my head high. *Anonymous* and my *Crew* had done our best for Michael Brown and the people of Ferguson, Missouri. Just as I predicted in the Anonymous speech to the Ferguson Million Mask March, Hacktivists would indeed be arrested and imprisoned for stupid long sentences under the draconian CFAA for their cyber actions in *Anonymous Operation Ferguson*. I spent the rest of the day tweeting, looking at the reams of protest pics and vids we had collected, and occasionally weeping. I cried a lot during this Op.

----------

I have tried my best in this Chapter of *Dark Ops* to reveal to the reader what it was like to be at the eye of a socio-political hurricane like *Anonymous Operation Ferguson*. To have your actions every day rippling out from your laptop in both space and time, and to have such profound consequences. Readers of my books and blog may be somewhat used to it, but what I want to close with is this simple fact: *Op Ferguson* easily topped them all so far. Hands down. *Anonymous Operation Ferguson* remains the single most intense actions I ever participated in within the context of either *Information Activism* in general, or *Anonymous* in particular. Just from a temporal standpoint of time, it was easily the longest continuously "hot" *Anonymous Operation* to date.

A year is a long time to go spending twelve hour days hopped up on adrenaline and caffeine, while you wage unseeable cyber war - receiving death threats daily from cops and patriot trolls. But huge innovations always take place in these long *Ops*, which is the pay-off. Future cyber armies of hacktivists will be fighting with the tools and techniques that we developed during the year of the *Ferguson Uprising*. Anonymous literally had changed the state of the art in cyber activism. Again.

*Anonymous* had also *been changed* itself by *Operation Ferguson*. Of course it goes without saying that is always the case with nearly every *Anonymous Operation*, but the changes this time were deep and profound - especially in the West and the USA. Topically, everything from the racial balance of hackers within *Anonymous USA*, to what sort of music would be the anthem and soundtrack of *Anonymous* going forward was altered irrevocably. I did learn to love hip hop and rap, but how could you not with a dear friend like my rap star Tef Poe.

There were deeper and more systemic changes within *Anonymous*. Some as I said in this Chapter, were technical, and mostly involved lessons in hacking tech and propaganda techniques - and especially as they relate to waging information warfare against police departments. Other changes in *Anonymous* from *Op Ferguson* were cultural. The previously socially acceptable 4chan term "nigga" became less prevalent. Overt racism, so long accepted within white western hacker underground culture began to become less popular. *Anonymous* was ten years old, and growing up.

It is to my mind a simple fact one can not deny, that *Anonymous Operation Ferguson* not only changed, but indeed helped to shape - the current iteration of the *Civil Rights Movement* known generically as *Black Lives Matter*. From the adoption of their transgressive and aggressive street protest tactics that were taught to them by Black Bloc Anarchists affiliated and directed by *Anonymous*, to the *BLM* concentration on information and digital tactics -

all were the direct influence of *Anonymous* on this new movement. Even culturally, black Americans now have a greater awareness of hacktivists in general, and *Anonymous* specifically - than I would have ever dreamed possible before *Anonymous Operation Ferguson*.

I have resisted the temptation in the years after *Anonymous Operation Ferguson* to morph the residual archived material and infrastructure into some "useful" and generic Op, like say Op BLM. Instead, the website www.OperationFerguson.cf remains online as a reminder that *Anonymous* is always watching. Police continue to kill unarmed black people at a staggering rate across the USA. But we will persist as a reminder to the tiny city of Ferguson, Missouri that if it ever happens again there - we *will* be back.

# EIGHT

## *Operation Anon Down*

-----------------------

*"I have stood upon the mountain called Anonymous, and looked down on a world inflamed with revolution."*

~~ Commander X

——————— • • • ———————

Thursday - July 16, 2015 approx. 9:00 AM ET - Starbucks Toronto, Ontario - CANADA

As I was settling into my day with a latte and a hopeful outlook, on the other side of Canada, thousands of kilometers away, a forty-eight year old *First Nations* man named James Daniel McIntyre, was protesting a local environmental issue near a restaurant in the tiny town of Dawson Creek, in British Columbia. What happened next will probably remain forever hotly disputed. But we know that like all of these types of incidents, it happened very fast.

There was some sort of disturbance inside the restaurant. It is alleged it was caused by James, and if this is true, was most likely protest related. Things escalated almost instantly, and RCMP was called. They had numerous cruisers in the area to cover the planned protest, and were there in seconds. An officer approached James Daniel McIntyre with his gun drawn, barked several orders that *Anonymous* came to believe James was attempting to comply with, when an instant later, he was gunned down. He bled out, moaning and screaming why did you shoot me, and then died. We believe it took him two minutes of agony to bleed out and die.

Why the fuck, you might ask, would this even come onto *my* radar, much less concern, me - sipping my latte thousands of kilometers to the east, as this tragic drama unfolded? Because when James Daniel McIntyre got himself blasted by the RCMP in Dawson Creek, BC that morning, he wasn't just any *First Nation* environmental protester. James Daniel McIntyre was wearing a *Guy Fawkes Mask*, and identified as a part of the idea called *Anonymous*. And that's why within minutes, and again as in *Anonymous Operation Ferguson*, other *Anons* and I found ourselves putting up an *Anonymous Operation* literally before they collected the body out of the street.

In this case, we decided that this being the third *Anon* killed at a protest wearing a *Mask* that we had cataloged over the years, the time had come to stand up a permanent *Op*.

**165**

And so that very moment was born *Anonymous Operation Anon Down*. Within an hour of James Daniel McIntyre death, we issued the following Press Release:

Anonymous Press Release: Operation Anon Down

Saturday - July 18, 2015 4:00 PM ET

At approximately 6:30 PM PT on July 17, 2015 at an Anonymous protest in Dawson Creek, British Columbia which the RCMP was informed about in advance, an RCMP officer mercilessly shot and killed a masked Anon without provocation or cause. The situation should have been handled according to Treaty 8 protocols. And, if Canadian police were as brave as Canadian nurses, they could deal with people with knives without hiding behind bullets. This is the fourth Anon to be slain by security forces around the world in as many years. Turkey, Egypt, Palestine and now British Columbia in Canada. As in the past, Anonymous will not stand idly by while our own are cut down in mask. Anonymous has fought for the lives of protesters all over the globe, from Tahir Square in Egypt to Ferguson, Missouri. We will most certainly avenge one of our own when they are cut down in the streets while protesting the earth wrecking environmental policies of the Canadian government.

To this end Anonymous announces the launch of Operation Anon Down. The focus of this Op going forward will be gaining justice (and vengeance if necessary) for our fallen comrade in Dawson Creek. But we will also memorialize our previously slain brethren, and prepare to take action for future Anons killed by police - as we have no doubt they will cut down more of us.

To begin we will identify the RCMP officer involved, thoroughly dox him - and release that dox on the Internet.

Because the world has a right to know every detail about killer cops. We will offer support and raise funds if necessary to cover the burial expenses of our fallen comrade. He will be buried with the honor and dignity that his courage has earned him. We will ensure that he is never forgotten, and takes his place in the growing ledger of brave Anonymous martyrs around the world. Then we will press the RCMP and Canadian government for justice. This RCMP officer must be named, fired, and charged - for the murder of our brother Anon. And if we do not receive justice, rest assured there will be revenge.

We call upon our fellow Anons in Canada to take to the streets and protest at the RCMP headquarters in every Province, every day - until our demands for justice are met. We call upon the Global Collective of Anonymous and allied crews to remove the RCMP cyber infrastructure from the Internet. March, create and sign petitions, hack, dox. We may not be able to bring back our fallen comrade, we may not even be able to prevent other Anons from being slain by murderous police - but we can sure as hell show them that there will be a steep price to pay when they kill us.

~~ Anonymous

----------

While mass protests never developed, *Anonymous Operation Anon Down* managed to inaugurate itself in style with a whole series of rather punishing hacks against the RCMP and CSIS, Canada's spy agency. The latter resulted in the exfiltration of a number of classified documents which were dumped. And in the end, despite the results of our exhaustive investigation proving that James Daniel McIntyre did not need to be shot to death this fateful day, the officer involved was exonerated.

What was born, however, was a new resolve on the part of *Anonymous* to keep *Operation Anon Down* fully active, to catalog and memorialize those already lost to us, and to fight for justice (or at least vengeance) for those who we know by now will fall in the future. Our very own *Wall Of Martyrs* was inaugurated at the new website www.OperationAnonDown.cf and *Anonymous* began to be more aware of the need to not just leave no one behind, but to bury our dead. Like I said, after a decade, *Anonymous* had finally grown up.

----------

Monday - August 24, 2015 approx. 9:00 AM ET - Second Cup Coffee House  Toronto, Ontario - CANADA

At the beginning of this book, President Obama had made the public threat that someday he may order a drone attack on a hacker. No one believed he'd ever do it. No one, that it is, outside of *Anonymous*. We always knew he would do it. People seem to think Democrats are our natural allies. Nothing could be further from the truth. Obama has locked up more leakers and hacktivists, for insanely long sentences, than all the previous US administrations combined. And Hillary Clinton actually joked about droning Julian Asange, founder of WikiLeaks, a hacker, and my *friend*. No, Democrats are definitely not our friends.

Today it was announced that President Obama had made good on his threat, and had ordered a drone attack on a former *Anon* and hacktivist who appeared earlier in this story, who went by the online name of Tr1cK. Tr1cK had slowly radicalized, transitioning out of *Anonymous* and into more transgressive Middle Eastern hacker circles. Not in and of itself enough to get one droned. But then Tr1cK did the stupidest thing possible, a decision that cost him his life. He joined ISIS.

They were so hurting for hackers they made him a Minister of Hackers or some such silly shit. And of course, they then announced this to the world. The next day there were headlines around the world about the ex-Anon who had joined ISIS. Fuck me, Tr1cK - what the fuck were you thinking my brother?

It took only a few months to nail down Tr1cK's location in Syria. The USA by then had hundreds of drones in the Syrian skies. Some of the details that follow have never been revealed publicly, and were discovered by myself in a secret investigation of Tr1cK's killing that I did in the aftermath. Tr1cK always traveled with his nephew, under the well-founded assumption that he would not be droned if he had a child with him. But on the day that would be his last, Tr1cK wanted a little bit of hashish to dull the suffering that living among ISIS caused. So he slipped into an alley behind the coffee house where he often connected to the Internet, to quickly score a gram of the Middle East's finest. He thought he would be fine, only gone a moment - out and back in. Out of propriety, he didn't want to bring his nephew out into the alley for a drug deal. That decision cost Tr1cK his life, and saved the life of his nephew.

Because seconds was all the drone silently loitering at twenty-thousand feet needed to lock onto Tr1cK's mobile (which he so foolishly forgot to leave behind), and fire a hellfire missile. As Tr1cK handed over a wad of Syrian currency and reached for the small package, the missile struck - turning my friend and comrade into pink mist. To say that I did not take it well would be a gross understatement. I was livid beyond words to describe. I was more than mad, I was *murderously* mad. I wanted blood for blood. And I let the world know it.

Tr1cK was ratted out by an American hacktivist turned FBI informant known as Sm00p. Sm00p, the founder of the detestable troll group *Rustle League*, had worn a wire to DefCon, gathering evidence on at least one American hacker who went to prison, another close friend of mine actually.

In the process she gathered enough intelligence from *Anons* at DefCon that DoD was able to find Tr1cK's location in Syria. Not only had the first hacker been officially droned, but he was ratted out by an American hacker *snitch*.

Now I understand what you, the reader, will be thinking. Ok, maybe he was a cool cat, but come on, the dude joined *ISIS*, right? Ok fine. That was a poor career choice on Tr1cK's part. I wish I had known he had slid so far, he respected me - I might have been able to stop him. But I will never accept living in a world where we drone hackers. No matter who they work for. If they knew where he was in Syria, then stalk him and arrest him. But I will never accept the extra-judicial assassination of hackers. Never. Fuck the USA and NATO.

----------

Friday - January 15, 2016 approx. 9:30 AM ET - Starbucks Toronto, Ontario - CANADA

Today I was working with the mother of an incarcerated Anon named Matt DeHart. Matt DeHart is an American citizen and former U.S. Air National Guard intelligence analyst known for his involvement with the Anonymous hacker group and WikiLeaks and claims to have received classified documents alleging serious misconduct by the CIA. He was indicted for alleged possession of indecent images from under-aged boys in 2010, but claims that this was a ruse in order to punish him for his online activities. A judge ruling on the case found this credible. He was however imprisoned for 21 months without access to proofs for these allegations. After being released on bond in 2012, he unsuccessfully sought asylum here in Canada, claiming he had been tortured by the FBI with regards to the classified documents. In November 2015 he struck a plea bargain to serve a 7 and a half year sentence.

Former whistleblower Jesselyn Radack, his supporters and DeHart himself purports the allegations are a ruse by the FBI to discredit him over the information he has released.

One of the details of Matt's case that has always bothered me is his description of his torture. I had discussed this with Matt's dad early on, and as I didn't really have any evidence, only a story, it really didn't help much. I'm telling it now in hopes that it may help vindicate Matt, and maybe even lighten his load a little as he serves out his hideous sentence in Federal prison in the USA should he read this book. It happened in late 2012 and into 2013. I received a series of three separate reports from *Anons* living in the Mid and South West of the USA.

They all described being "abducted" by Federal agents, taken to secure locations, tied to chairs, drugged, and slapped around and questioned. When it was over they were simply taken to where they were picked up and unceremoniously dumped. One individual claims he was questioned about the drug cartels in Mexico, the other two quite bizarrely claimed they were questioned about their *Anonymous* campaign to investigate the Illuminati! These agents were described not as standard issue fibs, but as "MIBs".

For obvious reasons, I dismissed these reports as fantasy. That is until I read the report of Matt DeHart's alleged torture. Tied to a chair, drugged with Thorazine, and beaten with a metal rod while being questioned about secret documents and WikiLeaks. Yeah....hard to buy that is a coincidence. One of my hugest regrets in all this was to dismiss those original reports as lunatic fantasies. There is apparently no length whatsoever that the government of the USA won't go in its war against *Anonymous*.

What I was working with Matt's mom today on was helping her set up an online support group for the family members of those *Anons* currently in harm's way. She and my sister intended to found it, and reach out to the other families of the *Anons* mentioned in this Chapter.

What does this say about our movement, that we need such things as support groups for our traumatized family members? I don't know. I try not to think about it too much, to be honest.

----------

Saturday - November 5, 2016 approx. 6:30 PM ET - Tim Hortons Toronto, Ontario - CANADA

Today was *Guy Fawkes Day* again, and yet another annual *Million Mask March*. This year a number of us influential *Anons* made the hard choice to keep the publicity very low key and muted. Frankly, I was afraid of a "terrorist" attack on a crowd of *Mask* wearing brothers and sisters. *Anonymous Operation ISIS*, while not really supported by most of the old-school influential Anons, had nevertheless been a resounding success at hurting ISIS where it counted most. Not on the battlefield, mind you, but in cyber space and the domain of information warfare. But it was still a shitty idea for an Anonymous Operation, and was as I said highly opposed by many influential Anons. Below is an article I wrote on this topic in March 2016:

My Enemies Enemy: Why Operation ISIS Is A Bad Idea For Anonymous

Over the course of this winter several Anon Cells and many individual Anons have participated in "Operation ISIS" also referred to as "Operation Paris". This massive and global Op successfully targeting ISIS, Al-Nursa, and Boko Harem has absorbed huge resources within the Global Collective, and held much of the world's attention riveted. To be clear, I am not debating in the least either this Op's scope, nor its effectiveness. What I will argue though, is that this Op is the single most damaging Op to ever have been launched by Anonymous.

**172**

In one of his recent communiques from a Federal penal colony in the USA, Jeremy Hammond laid out an incredibly cogent and powerful argument against the continued prosecution of Operation ISIS by Anonymous. I encourage you to pause and read the words of this brilliant Anarchist and faithful Anonymous participant:

*"The attacks in France were a terrible but unfortunately predictable response by desperate people who, after a decade of war and occupation, want the west to taste what we have been regularly dishing out. But we cannot allow them to be used to justify more war.*

*In the wake of the Paris attacks, the Western governments are provoking Islamophobic hatred in order to escalate military operations in the Middle East and push police state powers. It's a familiar script, and from prison, I've been following these developments, disturbed about the attacks on immigrant and Muslim communities and the resurgence of the fascist right.*

*I remember in the wake of 9/11, the waves of blind patriotism and xenophobia that the war-mongering politicians used to push police-state laws, mass surveillance, and rampant militarization. It was never about fighting terrorism or weapons of mass destruction, but about US empire: control over land, oil, and drug production, like all wars. Hundreds of thousands of innocents were murdered by the US military over the longest war in our history while we escalated drone warfare elsewhere in Syria, Yemen, Pakistan, and Somalia, creating the conditions which gave rise to ISIS in the first place.*

*That same post-9/11 hysteria is back and all the war-mongers are again frothing at the mouth with hate for immigrants and refugees, pushing for national Muslim registration databases, and for regime change in Syria.*

But I never thought Anonymous would join in on their frenzied call for war. Apparently, GhostSec and others purportedly associated with Anonymous have been DDoSing forums, taking down Twitter accounts, and reporting IP addresses to law enforcement in collaboration with shady military contractors like Kronos Advisory. The naïve fools behind the operation are being manipulated by intelligence agents taking advantage of the emotional reaction to the Paris attacks to harness our skills to fight their hypocritical "war on terrorism."

As someone who hacked with Anonymous and marched against the war in Iraq, I completely oppose #OpISIS and any attempts to co-opt our movement into supporting the government's militaristic agenda. Escalated US military involvement is certainly going to result in more civilian deaths, as it already has. All deaths of innocent civilians are a tragedy, and we cannot value one life over another. (And you are still more likely to be shot down by police than in a terrorist attack.)

The same intelligence industry that runs their own NSA hacker operations against ISIS uses the same counter-terrorism justification to spy on everyday civilians with no regards for rights to privacy, encryption, or anonymity. They have always targeted Anonymous and other dissident groups as terrorists, and when they aren't trying to discredit or imprison us, they are attempting to co-opt us – sometimes openly by attending conference like DEFCON, seducing us with promises of money or calls for patriotic duty, other times covertly lurking around IRC channels attempting to steer us unwittingly into supporting their agenda. Remember, Sabu asked me to hack government websites of Syria and Turkey, among others, which I did, unaware he was an FBI informant. They didn't want to talk about it at my sentencing hearing, but they did condemn my attacks against police and military contractors at length.

*The agents out there encouraging you to "hack the terrorists" will have no problem turning around and locking you up for years if you are not useful to their agenda.*

*We won't let Anonymous be unwittingly used to further the military industrial complex's imperialistic operations around the world. We don't work for the government – we are against all governments. We are on the side of the oppressed, not the oppressors. We support the victims of war, not the war-makers. If you want to report membership lists and IP addresses of suspected terrorists, go join the CIA or hang out with wannabes like Stratfor or the th3j35t3r. Call it state-sponsored hacking, patriotic hacktivism, whatever – just don't you dare call yourselves Anonymous.*

*I urge my comrades still out there in the trenches, sitting on some hot 0day, ready to loot databases and trash systems. If you want to stop war and terrorism, target who Martin Luther King Jr. called the "largest purveyor of violence in the word today" – the US government. So Anonymous, get to it – drone manufacturers, white hat infosec contractors, CIA directors, Donald Trump, and your local police department – they all have blood on their hands, they are all fair game."* ~~ Jeremy Hammond

In this incredible piece, Jeremy focuses on the effect Op ISIS has on world peace and the anti-war movement. This is the crux of his argument, and as I said it's powerful. Jeremy has mythic stature within the Global Collective of Anonymous, and his brutal indictment of Op ISIS is crucial to those of us active Anons who would like to see this ill-fated action wrapped up.

Lending their voices to this anti-Op ISIS camp, a group of very well respected and influential Anons recently released a joint statement:

*Hello World --*

*We are Anonymous. ISIS is small state that brutally censors visiting journalists and its own people. As such it must be opposed. The question is in what manner should it be opposed.*

*We think it's great if people want to hack ISIS and publish their secrets. But engaging in social media censorship campaigns and dealing with intelligence contractors and government agents is deeply stupid. The former will contribute to legitimize the spread of internet censorship and will lead to the increased censorship for everyone, including Anonymous. Dealing with government agents et al will not only result in many more informers in Anonymous bu twill also damage its reputation as it will lead to a view that Anonymous is too close to US intelligence interests.*

*The same intelligence industry that runs their own NSA hacker operations against ISIS uses the same counter-terrorism justification to spy on everyday civilians with no regards for rights to privacy, encryption, or anonymity. They have always targeted Anonymous and other dissident groups as terrorists, and when they aren't trying to discredit or imprison us, they are attempting to co-opt us – sometimes openly by attending conferences like DEFCON, seducing us with promises of money or calls for patriotic duty, other times covertly lurking around IRC channels attempting to steer us unwittingly into supporting their agenda.*

*We would like to strongly advise - while we cannot speak for the whole of Anonymous - to always release information to the public, as we want to operate in its interest.*

*Any attempts to act in secrecy, supporting political or governmental organizations, will be discouraged by us or completely ignored to safeguard our allies and supporters fighting for openness and transparency within governments, dictatorships and organizations around the globe that control various aspects of our lives.*

*We are on the side of the oppressed, not the oppressors. We support the victims of war, not the war-makers.*

~~ Anonymous

In this open letter, the ideas of Jeremy Hammond regarding the effect on the anti-war movement were expanded to begin to explore the idea that we are in fact aiding a virulent enemy by fighting that enemies battles for them. And since so much ground has already been covered by these other great Anons above I want to take this last point, which is embodied within my chosen title for this piece – and expand upon it at more length.

Because not only does Op ISIS aid the military-industrial complex, do harm to civilians – and weaken the anti-war movement. In addition to these things, Op ISIS also greatly assists the USA and NATO – both of whom are sworn enemies of Anonymous. In fact both the USA and NATO have actually classified the peaceful movement of Anonymous in the same category as ISIS, Al-Nursa and other radical jihadists. Amazing heroes like Jeremy Hammond and Barrett Brown are doing insane amounts of time in the USA Federal penal system, a system so brutal that several European countries will not extradite hackers to the USA anymore because their prisons fail to meet the minimum standards required by the UN Human Rights Accord.

So if we are at war with (and taking casualties from) NATO and the USA, and if Anonymous is as the Snowden leaks proved classified in the same category as ISIS by our enemies – then why on earth would we want to assist the USA and NATO in their war against these jihadists? Will this not simply free up NATO and USA resources that they can then turn against Anonymous, against us? In what way does this make any strategic sense at all? Will the USA pardon Hammond and Brown from gratitude? Will we even get a "thank you" from NATO? Of course not. President Obama knows all about Anonymous, and he and his administration hate us. NATO Central Command has called us the biggest danger to global stability in the world. These people want Anons either locked in a cage or dead.

*Op ISIS* is unethical, immoral – and damaging to world peace. It only aids the military industrial complex of the USA and NATO. It weakens Anonymous by aiding our enemies and giving our enemies another easy route by which to infiltrate us. I would guess over half of the "Anons" leading Op ISIS are in fact Federal law enforcement or intelligence agents. And the ample arguments put forth in this piece don't even begin to delve into the historical fact that the USA, through militaristic and diplomatic blundering – essentially created ISIS in the first place! Along with the other voices of Anonymous quoted in this piece, I add my own: let's end *Op ISIS* and let the USA and NATO battle their own monsters. At least until Jeremy and Barrett get their Presidential pardons. Then we'll talk.

----------

I spent the day in my new role as a Team Member of the *Free Lauri Love Campaign* being run out of the UK. Lauri Love is a Finnish-British activist charged extraterritorially with stealing data from United States Government computers including the US Army, Missile Defense Agency, and NASA via computer intrusion.

Love is under indictment in the United States (2013 in District of New Jersey, 2014 in Southern District of New York and Eastern District of Virginia). As of 2016, the United States is trying to extradite him to America to face charges and he is fighting the extradition. The National Crime Agency (UK) arrested Love in 2013. In February 2015, the BBC revealed that Love was taking legal action for the return of computers seized by the National Crime Agency (NCA) when he was arrested. This past May, Judge Nina Tempia of the Westminster Magistrates' Court ruled that Love did not have to tell the National Crime Agency (United Kingdom) what his passwords, or encryption keys, are.

So essentially, Lauri encrypted his drives with full-disk encryption, hacked a bunch of fed networks in the USA, and when the cops in the UK said to unlock his drives he gave them the finger, then had the moxie to even sue them to get the computers back. If you read this Lauri, it's because of you that I finally took the time to implement full-disk encryption. Because that shit is straight up hysterical. As of this printing the USA is still fighting to extradite Lauri Love to the USA to stand trial under their brutal CFAA law. Lauri has at least one last appeal left.

----------

Monday - November 10, 2016 approx. 9:30 AM ET  - Tim Hortons North York, Ontario - CANADA

On February 17th of this year, an article popped up in my feeds that caught my attention. It was by Esquire magazine, and the headline could not help but stop any hacktivist and make them curious. Now..., yeah. So that seems pretty bizarre, right? As I read the piece, I recalled seeing the news of the Anonymous cyber-attacks against the Boston Children's Hospital a couple of years ago.

I also remembered not being terribly happy that Anonymous was attacking a hospital. Of course like most people, I didn't even bother to read up on exactly why Anons were attacking a children's hospital. And this is the problem when we jump to conclusions without even researching what is really going on.

So, let's first turn this moral dilemma on its head for a second and see where we go. If you have solid evidence that a hospital is torturing children, no like seriously, torturing little kids, and you want to protest this fact – what is the least disruptive method to patient care? You have basically two options to start, so let's examine them thoughtfully. You can call for in-the-streets protest and march with ten thousand on the hospital. Perfectly legal to do that. Some may go to jail briefly, but they'll be out in hours. But what about that pesky disruption to patient care everyone has their panties in a bunch over? Well, trying to get ambulances and emergency supplies through all those packed streets seems pretty disruptive to patient care to me.

Now, let's say you go the route that *Anonymous* chose – and protest online. *Anonymous* chose its targets with surgical precision, taking out only symbolic pages like the donations portal, etc.. By the hospital's own admission, this did not in the least affect patient care. And this online protest cost the hospital far less in "damages" than cleaning up after street marches would have. And so now, as we examine this deeper we see that the actions of Anonymous on those seven fateful days in 2014 were actually pretty reasonable, given what was being protested.

So what does any of this have to do with Martin Gottesfeld the Anon mysteriously arrested by the FBI after being rescued by a Disney Cruise ship? Plenty. The same US prosecutor who drove our dear Aaron Swartz to suicide is accusing Marty of being the orchestrator and manager of the Anonymous Operation which targeted the Boston Children's Hospital over the barbaric treatment of vulnerable sick children.

Something for which he deserves a reward for if true, but instead he faces 15 years in prison thanks to the persecution of Information Activists by the USA using the archaic and ridiculous CFAA.

Those who know my own story know that I have been running and hiding in Canada for 5 years, attempting to escape this exact same persecution of Anons and hacktivists in the USA. And it may perhaps be true that Marty G was on that sailboat attempting to also flee the same persecution in the USA. If so, it's a damn shame his boat failed him. And Marty G is far from the first Anon to seek to become a political dissident and ex-patriot. I was the first to publicly do so five years ago. Shortly after Matt DeHart and his family also entered Canada, albeit legally – in an ultimately unsuccessful bid to have the Canadian authorities grant him political asylum. At least one other very well known and influential Anon has publicly announced they were going into self-imposed political exile in Europe preemptively – before being charged with anything! America's best and brightest are fleeing the jack-booted secret police in the middle of the night in ever increasing numbers.

But where many would have seen failure and defeat, Martin Gottesfeld saw yet another opportunity to protest. This time, he decided to protest on behalf of all Anonymous and Information Activists being persecuted in the USA via the CFAA. And the form of protest this young hero chose will send shivers up your spine, at least if you have any humanity. Because Marty G is at this writing 40 days into a hunger strike to defend our right in the USA to protest peacefully online. Read his statement below, issued on the day he was formerly indicted under the CFAA:

*"The fact that Ortiz's office indicted on debate day, and without a press release, shows they are aware of the unconscionable human rights violations they are attempting to sweep under the rug and the precedence of impunity that would be even more firmly established.*

*They have no compassion for the suffering of Justina Pelletier, a mentally and physically challenged child, ripped from her family, left in agony without her painkillers, and locked in an abusive psych ward. Nor are they concerned with any real semblance of true justice. They hope to pursue this case far from public scrutiny and also without any mention how they caused the death of Aaron Swartz. Now their opponent is an imprisoned human rights activist on the third week of a hunger strike, and they still won't engage in a public debate where they hold every advantage, except the whole truth. This indictment, and the manner in which it was unsealed, were cowardly acts."*

~~ Martin Gottesfeld

There are two forms of transgressive protest that are so extreme they have always given me the creeps. Self-immolation, and hunger striking. The obvious reason is that you have to be pretty desperate and disenfranchised to even attempt such forms of protest. But the other reason, at least vis a vis hunger striking – is more personal. You see, I tried a hunger strike. Once. Only once. And I failed miserably. I lasted three lousy days and in the end I was begging a jail guard for a candy bar at three in the morning. I didn't have the courage then, and I know damn well now that I never will. Unless you have fasted or otherwise gone without food for even a day or two, you can not begin to comprehend the utter agony you endure when hunger striking. This is a form of protest so severe that one is compelled to respect it. The fact that Marty G is doing this for us, for Anonymous, for all of our right to protest online in the USA – this seems to me to warrant the undivided attention of the entire *Global Collective*, as well as all people around the world of good conscience who value free speech on the Internet.

I decided that since Marty had placed himself in harm's way, and since if he died of the hunger strike we would need to add him to our *Wall Of Martyrs*, *Anonymous Operation Anon Down* would be an appropriate venue to try and raise the Global Collective consciousness on his case. As such on November 4, 2016 (the day before *Guy Fawkes Day*), we issued the following Press Release on Martin Gottesfeld, one of our own:

Anonymous Operation Anon Down Press Release: SOS Issued To Global Collective As Anon On Hunger Strike Nears Death

Monday - November 4, 2016  2:15 PM ET

Greetings World --

In 2014 Anonymous launched Operation Justina to defend a young girl who was being held prisoner and tortured by the Boston Children's Hospital. A series of DdoS attacks and other online actions lasting approximately one week were launched by Anonymous to bring attention to this poor girl's situation. The strikes were surgical in nature, targeting only symbolic parts of the vast Boston Children's Hospital's network - such as donation portals, etc. Patient care was not even slightly affected by these online protests.

On February 17th of this year, Marty Gottesfeld and his wife were rescued at sea by a Disney Cruise Lines vessel and immediately Marty was taken into custody by the FBI for orchestrating and participating in the online protests against the Boston Children's Hospital during Op Justina two years prior. But for Marty Gottesfeld this was simply another opportunity to protest injustice, in this case - the political targeting of Information Activists in general, and Anons in particular - using the archaic and brutal Computer Fraud & Abuse Act.

And so in defense of the idea we call Anonymous, and facing the same barbaric US Prosecutor Carmen Ortiz who drove our dear Aaron Swartz to his death three years ago, Marty Gottesfeld went on a hunger strike.

You can read the detailed story as well as Marty G's full statement upon embarking on his hunger strike below. -->

https://thecryptosphere.com/2016/08/31/freemartyg-operation-announced-for-marty-gottesfeld-alleged-anonymous-hacker/

Marty Gottesfeld is now past the 40 day mark with no food, and as of this Friday - November 11th, after being placed arbitrarily into isolation, Marty has also decided to abstain from fluids. At this juncture he may not have long to live, and yet the Federal Bureau of Prisons refuses to transport Marty Gottesfeld to the hospital where he can receive the constant medical monitoring someone in his condition needs. Solitary confinement is an act of torture according to the UN Human Rights Accord and other applicable international law. This is unacceptable, and Anonymous will not stand for this.

Anonymous now issues the following demands:

1) We demand that Marty Gottesfeld be IMMEDIATELY transported to the nearest hospital and that he be given the best medical treatment available.

2) We demand that the White House send an envoy to visit Marty Gottesfeld while he is still conscious to discuss the demands he has issued as part of his hunger strike.

3) We demand that the USDOJ treat Marty Gottesfeld with true compassion and justice, and either reduce or remove these charges - because protesting online should never have such severe penalties attached to it. The sole purpose of these exorbitant charges is to attack and chill the speech and actions of Anonymous. This is the very definition of political persecution. And while this war by USDOJ against Anonymous is not new, we draw the line at Marty G. Enough is enough.

Anonymous calls upon the world, all its people's and leaders - to rise to Marty Gottesfeld defense. Visit the website's, follow the Twitter accounts - and participate in all the announced Action Alerts. Spread the word, write in your blogs, contact journalist friends, and tweet non-stop. Do not allow this young man's heroic sacrifice to go un-noticed.

To our fellow Anons in the Global Collective of Anonymous. Every nation, city, and Crew: This is an SOS. Marty Gottesfeld is starving himself to death, and is near death even now - because he is standing for us, for all Anonymous, and especially for those Anons who have been victims of the pogrom against Information Activists in the USA. We may not be able to save Marty's life. In the end it is his to give for the cause. But we can not only stand with him now in his final days, we can also seek our vengeance if US Prosecutor Carmen Ortiz takes him from us as she did Aaron Swartz. Follow and spread the Action Alerts. Check out the Operational Information page on the Op Anon Down website for USDOJ and prison targets. Remember the most important demand is to get Marty to a hospital permanently so he can be closely monitored. Until then the pressure must be relentless.

ACTION ALERTS:

1) Write to and Tweet at world leaders and try and get their attention to support Marty Gottesfeld. From the Pope and the Dali Lama to Birgitta Jonsdottir MP in Iceland. try and convince them to get President Obama to intervene to save Marty's life.

2) If you are a US citizen, write to your Federal representatives and ask them to intervene in Marty Gottesfeld defense.Here are some resources that will make this very easy. -->

https://www.nationalpriorities.org/take-action/contact-your-representative/

http://letter2congress.rallycongress.com/698/

http://www.house.gov/representatives/find/

3) Participate in the Perpetual Twitter Tsunami: Most of you have heard of Twitter Storms. Well, this is like that except signal-boosted through the roof because of the dire nature of the situation. Oh, and it never ends until Marty Gottesfeld is safe. Tweet non-stop, DAY AND NIGHT. Do not be afraid or ashamed, this young man is giving his life for Anonymous before our eyes. Saturate Twitter with his cause. Re-tweet, copy-paste Tweets, and compose originals. Do not worry about trending hashtags, as we are going for deep penetration as opposed to a brief topic trends. But more than anything, be relentless. As relentless at least as US Prosecutor Ortiz is.

4) Write to Marty, let him know how much support he has. FLOOD him with letters of love and kindness:

http://www.freemartyg.com/support-marty.html

5) Visit the Free Marty G website often and click the Support link for more ways to help including petitions, donations, etc.

Finally, for those ships in Anonymous that are equipped with cannons. Check out the Operational Information page for details on prison and USDOJ targets and attack them relentlessly with one demand: transport Marty Gottesfeld to the hospital IMMEDIATELY and allow him to be cared for and monitored by medical professionals. Until that demand is met, attack the targets without quarter.

Anonymous has been at war with the USA government since it first attacked us in 2011. And we will continue to prosecute this war against this evil empire without mercy. You may hunt us, cage us, and even kill us - but you can't stop us. And you will pay a price not even measurable in dollars.

We Are Anonymous

We Are Everywhere

We Are Legion

We Do Not Forgive

We Do Not Forget

Expect Us

-------------------

Op Anon Down Site: www.OperationAnonDown.cf

Free Marty G Site:  www.FreeMartyG.com

FreeAnons Site:  www.FreeAnons.org

Twitter Accounts:

@FreeMartyG

@OpAnonDown2015

@FreeAnons

----------

After 100 days, Marty Gottesfeld ended his hunger strike, much to everyone's relief. He is still facing charges and is in prison as this book goes to print. He is facing over a decade. The child abusers he exposed have yet to even be investigated.

----------

With the completion of this, my second book - the story of my involvement in the *Anonymous Global Collective* is more or less up-to-date. *Behind The Mask: An Inside Look At Anonymous* and *Dark Ops: Anon Anonymous Story* take in a total of eight years that I was a part of the idea called *Anonymous*. During those eight years, I spent six of them on the run from the *FBI Cyber Crime Division*, and five of those years in hard political exile here in Canada. *Anonymous* itself is a mere ten years old, so I had played my role throughout the majority of its history. It is perhaps instructive to pause briefly and take a step back to view the panoramic picture of what exactly this idea called *Anonymous* had become in the past decade.

To begin, let us examine the broad state of the *Global Collective of Anonymous* as it stands ten years out. We have currently identified some *100 National Cells of Anonymous* worldwide, with approximately 2.5 million active participants. To be included in this list we looked for three primary criteria: a stylized and unique national logo, an active Twitter account – and a website of some sort. Now obviously, *National Cells* such as *Anonymous Afghanistan* or *Anonymous Vietnam* are quite likely very small – consisting of perhaps a few dedicated individuals in those countries. But others, especially in Africa (check out *Anonymous Kenya*) or South America (see the amazing *Anonymous Venezuela*) are some of the largest *National Cells* in our *Global Collective* – and are very active and effective politically within their country's sphere. And even more amazing is that many of these "third world" National Cells dwarf their western counterparts such as *Anonymous USA* or *Anonymous UK*.

In the past year we have seen some truly epic and historic *Anonymous Operations* conducted by these incredible National Cells of Anonymous working together or on their own. These *Ops* have truly had a magnificent impact politically and socially. From *Operation Ferguson* in the USA (www.OperationFerguson.cf) to *Anonymous Honduras* recent Operation No More Corruption that managed to bring down their government in about a month – *Anonymous* is making its might felt all across the world this year more powerfully than ever. In the past couple of years *Anonymous Philippines* has been so successful both online and in the streets that they have quite dramatically changed the political dynamic in that country, leaving their government in tatters and quite afraid of this enormously powerful *National Cell*. *Anonymous Palestine*, while it is a compact *National Cell* has not only been battering Israel over the Occupation – but they even had enough resources to spare that they were able to be extremely helpful to *Anonymous Operation Ferguson* in its early weeks last year.

And in a strange twist, *Anonymous Operation ISIS* led by the powerful allied crew *Ghost Security* has been more effective in the past year at denying these terrorists access to the Internet and social media than all the world's intelligence and law enforcement agencies combined! An incredible feat for a small group of hacktivists with almost no funding. No assessment of the current state of Anonymous would be complete without an examination of certain conflicts currently raging within or between a few of the National Cells. First a general word about conflict within *Anonymous*. It should not surprise anyone that in a massive global movement based at least in part on cyber warfare, that at some point a bit of in-fighting will break out. Not only is this inevitable, but it is sometimes good for the movement in the long-term as it serves as practice for when we turn our sights on the governments and corporations.

The first of these conflicts we'll look at, and one that has been in the media a bit lately – is the battle that has been raging for many years between *Anonymous Pakistan* and *Anonymous India*. This battle is primarily fought over the political issue revolving around the Kashmir. While *Anonymous India* seems to have the upper hand in these ongoing skirmishes, and thus still has a little energy left to actually challenge corruption and tyranny within their own country – both *National Cells* are almost exclusively engaged in this internecine conflict. In any case, neither *National Cell* is of any use whatsoever to the rest of the *Global Collective of Anonymous*, being completely consumed by this conflict and leaving both of these National Cells essentially paralyzed.

The other notable conflict is the seemingly perpetual battle between an insignificant number of 4chan trolls and haters who are still upset that the social justice activists essentially stole some of their memes and used them to create the *Anonymous Global Collective* we have today, and the *Anons* in *Anonymous USA*. This long simmering and rather one sided conflict has been ongoing since *Op Chanology* in 2008,

- and flares up again from time to time as the 4chan trolls and associated haters reach a crescendo of butt hurt at their complete lack of significance in the world. The conflict is limited to the *Anonymous USA National Cell*, and the vast majority of *Anons* worldwide are actually oblivious to it. This year, through the usual devious means and some lucky hacking – the 4chan idiots and their cadre of trolls and haters managed to cripple a couple of major domestic Ops in the USA – including *Operation Ferguson*.

The confusion and dis-information this conflict has generated has more or less rendered *Anonymous USA* paralyzed and diminished it to virtual insignificance within the overall *Global Collective* for the time being. While this sucks for the Anons in the USA, it really has not had any major effect on the *Global Collective of Anonymous* due to the simple fact that it has been many years since Anonymous USA was even relevant within *Anonymous* worldwide. One has only to look at the number of attendees at several of the third world *Million Mask Marches*, such as Manila and Caracas (many thousands in each city) – and compare those with the paltry 300 at the White House to see the truth in this. Many Anons have tried to call for "peace" within *Anonymous USA*, but it is my opinion this can not be achieved. You can not negotiate a peace with nihilistic terrorist trolls who are the very antithesis of everything Anonymous stands for. Only when the *Anons* in the USA learn how to ostracize, isolate – and render inert these cancerous individuals so as to protect their Ops from their destructive acts and corrosive influence will *Anonymous USA* begin to thrive and grow and once again become a functioning part of the *Global Collective*. This can be done, but that's a topic for another article entirely.

These internecine conflicts involving a few *National Cells* aside, the overall state of the *Anonymous Global Collective* is….astounding. Consider that a mere ten years ago Anonymous consisted of maybe ten thousand participants in two hazily defined *National Cells* (*Anonymous USA* & *Anonymous UK*).

A decade later we have, as mentioned above – an estimated 2.5 million participants in 100 National Cells. From the *Freedom Ops* of the "Arab Spring" to the recent downfall of the President of Honduras, *Anonymous* has been wielding geo-political power on a scale that is epic and historic for an essentially anarchic and decentralized political movement. *Anonymous* may be only an idea, but a decade after it was crystallized it may well have become the most powerful idea in human history.

But every powerful idea has a price, usually one paid in human blood and tears. The fact that we even needed an *Operation* like *Anonymous Operation Anon Down*, to catalog our martyrs, is testament to the obvious fact that we were not in Kansas anymore. And this evolution in the *Anonymous Global Collective* mirrored my own personal growth and understanding as well. I spent the vast majority of my life thinking of myself as a simple activist and coder. Now, I had somehow morphed from cyber protester to *cyber warlord*. And the persona, *Commander X*, had gone from being a simple way to identify myself in the Underground, to an international symbol of cyber resistance. I won't lie, being a symbol is not easy. Waging information war against Empires was not exactly how I envisioned spending the Autumn and Winter of my life.

In the end, it is my belief that what *Anonymous* is, is rather simple to explain. *Anonymous* is an idea. *Anonymous* is righteous indignation made manifest. *Anonymous* is simply something that happens whenever governments mess up too badly. It isn't even a new thing, far from it - it's ancient. *Anonymous* is as old as men using the *Mask of Anonymity* to challenge power. You can even trace the phenomenon back to the ancient *Mask Cults* of the stone ages. In the Middle Ages, men kept alive scientific knowledge by cloaking it in the *Old Mystery Schools*, where secrecy and anonymity protected scientific advances from a hysterical Church. *Anonymous* is nothing more than the modern cyber version of this age old idea of challenging authority from behind a *Mask*.

For this reason alone, I can promise you *Anonymous* is not going anywhere. It is as perennial as man himself.

Anonymous is a movement, that much is clear from my books. But one thing that gets short shrift, even in my tomes, is the fact that Anonymous is also a culture. It has an *ethos* and a *mythos*. It has *iconography* that lends meaning, and forms community via common recognition. It is the first of its kind in modern times pure *culture of resistance*. That common bond, combined with the formidable geo-political power that *Anonymous* wields - virtually ensures that people in power will be dealing with *Anonymous* for at least the next century. Maybe considerably longer. It has been the greatest honor of my life to be a small part of getting something that amazing started.

In addition to my own books on *Anonymous*, I would like to recommend a couple of others. The first is a short tome simply entitled *We Are Anonymous* by journalist Parmy Olson. The scene in which I appear in her book with security expert Aaron Barr is absolutely hysterical. The second book I can not recommend enough is entitled *Hacker, Hoaxer, Whistleblower, Spy: The Many Faces Of Anonymous* by anthropologist Gabriella Coleman. She also included a powerful anecdote that readers of my own books will recognize, involving my escape to Canada. I feel strongly enough that you should read this tome if you are interested in *Anonymous,* that I am including here a review I wrote of it back in 2014:

What It's Like To Be Studied By An Anthropologist: A Review Of "Hacker, Hoaxer, Whistleblower, Spy" By Gabriella Coleman

Before I launch into this, my very first ever book review – a couple of caveats are in order. First, I am and have been for 5 years – a very active part of the idea called Anonymous (which is the topic of Gabriella Coleman's book). I spend on average of 12 hours a day seven days a week working on various Operations and other Anonymous related projects.

My second caveat is that over the past five years as Biella, as she is fondly known within the Global Collective of Anonymous – wrote this work we became more than subject being studied and anthropologist. We became friends. The truth is that I, like many Anons – have grown quite fond of Biella. Unlike Parmy Olson, who despite putting one or two (more or less truthful) anecdotes about me in her own tome on Anonymous (but never made any attempt to speak with me) – Biella was a regular, even daily – part of not only my own life but the vast majority of active Anons globally. Not only was she already present in virtually every IRC channel I might enter in a day, but she would appear in moments as if by magic after I created a new channel for an Anonymous action or Op. This constant presence, combined with her witty, sweet – and truly nice personality made it almost impossible not to love Gabriella Coleman.

That said, I was totally prepared to be disappointed with "Hacker, Hoaxer, Whistleblower, Spy" after Parmy Olson's thoroughly wretched book on Anonymous (which actually wasn't even about Anonymous, but an unrelated off-shoot called LulzSec) soured me to books being accurately written about us. However, when I finally finished it and set it down about a week ago – I was stunned into a deep introspection that lasted quite a few minutes. To say that Biella's book was amazing is to admit that words simply fail to capture how I felt in those moments after I finished reading it. The closest thing I have ever felt was sitting in the world premiere of the full length motion picture documentary about Anonymous entitled "We Are Legion" (held in Toronto, and ironically I was sitting in the VIP section next to Biella). When you are involved in a history making and world changing endeavor, and you see or read about it accurately portrayed – there is a weird sense that overcomes you that is quite impossible to describe. It's a strange combination of awe and contemplation akin to "did we really do all that shit?".

It is definitely bizarre to read books or watch movies about something that has literally become the culmination of your entire life's work.

"Hacker, Hoaxer, Whistleblower, Spy" is both epic and encyclopedic. Not an easy combination to get right in a single work – but Coleman accomplishes it with a seeming ease that belies how incredibly difficult I know this task was for her. The work is epic in the sense that it succeeds brilliantly in capturing not only the historic moments of triumph within Anonymous, but the beautiful yet difficult to capture mythos and ethos of Anonymous. As an anthropologist, Biella is uniquely qualified to assimilate and then explain to the reader how Anonymous is not only a powerful and historic movement, but an incredibly rich and deep culture.

And Coleman's book is encyclopedic as a result of her sheer and unrelenting commitment. The number of hours that Biella spent immersed in Anonymous are quite simply incalculable. No one has ever made such an effort, and it is unlikely anyone ever will again. To put it simply Gabriella Coleman made herself a trusted and constant fixture in Anonymous for at least the entire five years that I have been involved. While I did note one or two secrets we managed to keep from her, there was virtually no corridor within the maze of Anonymous that Biella did not have access to.

The first thing I noticed as Biella handed me my signed copy of "Hacker, Hoaxer, Whistleblower, Spy" in her cramped and rather disorganized office space at McGill University (and yes, there was a Guy Fawkes mask resting on a shelf) was the size of the volume. It is fucking huge! As I idly flipped through it at that meeting whilst we had a wide-ranging conversation mostly centered on current Anonymous Operations, I noted it is a well crafted book. The font is very readable, and the tome is easy to navigate.

As I began to plow through it after that meeting I could see why Coleman chose the theme of a maze for the work. But let the reader relax, Biella is going to lead you through the maze that is Anonymous with charm, wit – and grace.

As I continued reading a couple of things leaped out at me. The first was the difference between a book about Anonymous written by a journalist and one written by an anthropologist. Journalists are expected to keep a decent amount of detachment from their subject matter, but the exact opposite is true of anthropologists. They are, in fact – expected to (within certain guidelines) immerse themselves in the culture they are studying to a very deep degree. This is why Coleman is not only allowed, but is commended – for "crossing the line" and in fact becoming Anonymous. As such she is able to go where no other commentator on Anonymous has gone before, and give a glimpse into our psyche, our hearts – even dare I say it but… our souls. Some of the barbs and witticisms she popped out fairly took me by surprise, and I actually had to read back and think – did she actually just say that OMG!

The other thing that blew my mind as I read Biella's book is the incredible historical depth, breadth and accuracy. And it was here that Coleman actually teaches me a thing or two about Anonymous. As one of the most active participants in Anonymous, working daily for five years with Anons from all over the world – I sort of thought I knew most everything that goes on in the Collective. But after reading "Hacker, Hoaxer, Whistleblower, Spy" I came to realize that however big a channel I may think I am burrowing through Anonymous, and no matter how lofty my view of the Global Collective – I am but a spec; one ant tunneling through a truly gigantic maze of a movement.

I won't give any spoilers. I am mentioned twice in the book by name, and the two episodes described were ones that were truly epic and memorable for me.

So I am well pleased with my own portrayal in this gigantic work. And I would like to thank Gabriella Coleman from the bottom of my heart for the incredibly kind mention she made of me in the Acknowledgments. As I have already stated, Biella has become one of my dearest friends in the movement – and it is a moment of huge pride to think that I helped her in any way to produce this wonderful and historic work.

And now, just so my readers don't think that I am a complete sycophant for Coleman and her book – I do have one fairly significant criticism. And it requires me to wade into a rather nasty controversy that involves another close friend of mine, Barrett Brown. As some may know, Barrett recently released his own review of Biella's book which, too put it lightly – was scathing. In the title of his review, as well as ad nauseum in the body – Brown uses the word libel to describe Coleman's treatment of him in "Hacker, Hoaxer, Whistleblower, Spy". Now, to be perfectly fair to both of my friends, that is in fact a form of libel on Barrett's part. Libel requires both deception as well as malicious intent. Gabriella Coleman is utterly incapable of either of these, and as such Barrett's claims of libel are frankly bullshit.

That said, I have to admit that I was rather disappointed with Biella's treatment of Barrett Brown – and her portrayal of his overall accomplishments within Anonymous. Again, being cautious of spoilers for the reader – I won't get into great detail or cite specific examples. Let's suffice to say that Coleman gives inordinate amount of time and credit to a rather tiny and insignificant group of nay-sayers in Anonymous who are familiar to all of us who have, like Brown – worked so hard to build Anonymous into the powerful social justice movement it has become.

Biella conversely seems to have missed many of Barrett's great achievements within Anonymous, as well as his popular appeal amongst the rank and file and his trusted status among those in Anonymous who wield global influence. It is not the only place in her book that Coleman seems to fall into the trap of giving this tiny group, which completely lacks any significant influence within Anonymous – an over-sized voice and role. Her treatment of certain "crews" within the orbit of Anonymous is also tainted with what I consider to be an erroneous focus on these perpetual "trolls" that plague the underside of Anonymous like fleas on a camel's belly.

But while this criticism is probably exaggerated for me due to the fact that it involves two close friends for whom I hold unfathomable affection, it is rather minuscule given the immense undertaking and achievement that is "Hacker, Hoaxer, Whistleblower, Spy". My reading of it was careful, slow – even painstaking at times as I scanned back often. Despite my dislike for a couple of choices in focus – I found not a single inaccuracy that I am certain of. In fact, despite its approximately 500 pages – I think I ran across only one typo. An incredible feat of editing given the size of the tome.

Overall, I find it incredibly unlikely given the amount of time, effort – and expertise that went into the creation of "Hacker, Hoaxer, Whistleblower, Spy" that anyone will publish anything even close to as comprehensive and thorough on the subject of Anonymous in the coming decades. Gabriella Coleman has accomplished the nearly impossible task of describing for the world who we are, what we do, what we did, and why – and does so in a way that if you are patient is comprehensible. Even her Conclusion, which in most lengthy academic works would be barely worth reading – Biella's prose is quite literally soaring.

She exits the maze she has patiently led you through, climbs a rickety stack of old books, spreads little angel wings and carries the reader with her into the great unknown, leaving the reader staring at *Anonymous*....and the future, with complete wonder and awe.

----------

As I reach the end of my story, and prepare to bid the reader ado (for now) - the obvious question seems to be "what is next?". For either myself or *Anonymous*, my answer is the same: I have not the slightest fucking idea. It would seem that quite literally anything is possible. We live in a world that has become so surreal that I am no longer even mildly surprised by what happens. We started this book with my Crew and I attempting to wreck the US Election in 2012, only to change our minds and instead preserve its integrity against a GOP hack and save the election for Obama. Fast forward four years, and the hacktivists ended up working against Hillary Clinton and in favor of Donald Trump. It would take another book just to explain how we got here from there.

Josh Corman said it best in the great documentary *We Are Legion*:

*"Nameless, faceless folks are having geo-political impact. It's both exhilarating to realize that, and terrifying. I guess it sort of depends on how that power is wielded."*

And that's what these books have been about for me. An accounting of how those of us who started this idea called *Anonymous* chose to use the moment history presented us with. Not all of our choices were either good or smart. In some cases we made more of a mess of things than we helped. There was collateral damage, innocents just caught in the cross-fire of an *Anonymous* cyber strike. There *are* a few regrets, I can not lie.

Being a *Cyber War Lord* is not easy, and I am only a human being in the end. I know I have always tried to do what I felt was right for humanity and our planet, to which my ultimate loyalty lies.

I do get a sense looking forward that the story is far from finished, and that *Anonymous* is only now hitting its stride. As this book goes to print tens of thousands of *Anons* are in the streets of Venezuela, and on the Internet, bringing down their own dictatorship. WikiLeaks continues the *Vault 7* release of basically the entire CIA hacking manual, plus code. Their entire arsenal, really. And already hackers are turning those tools against them in punishing cyber strikes on government and civilian targets.

One thing that people ask about a lot is my lifestyle in political exile. The key thing is I *move*, constantly. And I use every possible encryption and anonymization tool I can. Coffee house to coffee house, city to city, Province to Province. After over five years of this, I am exhausted. But it is what is necessary to keep me safe from the oppressors. My Team and I continue to search for a way to gain legal asylum in either a third country, or here in Canada. The prospects, while not nil, are grim. It looks as though I will be on the run a while longer.

When faced with implacable evil and oppressive power, we must never surrender. This has been the guiding principle of my life. Fate and my own early luck at being a childhood geek has placed me in the incredibly unique position of being able to make a true difference in this world, and in real-time. This is not an opportunity my nature will allow me to pass by, and so....it is what it is, I guess. But I am getting stronger, and my enemy - the government of the USA is getting weaker. Indeed, they are now in complete inner turmoil and paralyzed, and in part due to my actions against them. And so long as there is breath in my body and my mind is sound, I will fight against the evil and powerful of this world with every weapon at my disposal.

*"I walk the face of earth once more,*
*a mindless puppet, my strings are torn.*
*the creaky bones, the bad eyesight,*
*yet the chance to turn wrong to right.*
*wars-a-waging, old mans guilt,*
*the worlds now on more then just a tilt.*
*parents weeping, children slain,*
*bloody thoughts, fear will reign.*
*I look in the shadows, a creature did lurk,*
*he whispered to me, hiding a smirk.*
*"Thou shalt be killed if thee can't find,*
*the demon lurking in thou mind."*
*So off I ventured, to quench my thirst,*
*of corpses piled with hearts-a-burst.*
*And on that quest what did I see?"*
~~ Joseph


*"In times of trouble and insanity*
*I carry masks to disguise*
*the pain I carry*
*secure behind my eyes*

*I can never let out again*
*the misery I hide*
*to hell with my dignity*
*to hell with my pride*

*from this day forward*
*and for ever more*

*I will mount this mask*
*that will be my lore*

*No reaching out when I am weak*
*no solace will I seek*

*when you look for answers*
*when you say your prayers*
*all you will see is masks*
*and no pain that I bare"*
*~~ Joe Dirt*


*"My first thought was, he lied in every word,*
*That hoary cripple, with malicious eye*
*Askance to watch the working of his lie*
*On mine, and mouth scarce able to afford*
*Suppression of the glee, that pursed and scored*
*Its edge, at one more victim gained thereby.*

*What else should he be set for, with his staff?*
*What, save to waylay with his lies, ensnare*
*All travellers who might find him posted there,*
*And ask the road? I guessed what skull-like laugh*
*Would break, what crutch 'gin write my epitaph*
*For pastime in the dusty thoroughfare,*

*If at his counsel I should turn aside*
*Into that ominous tract which, all agree,*
*Hides the Dark Tower. Yet acquiescingly*
*I did turn as he pointed: neither pride*
*Nor hope rekindling at the end descried,*
*So much as gladness that some end might be.*

For, what with my whole world-wide wandering,
What with my search drawn out thro' years, my hope
Dwindled into a ghost not fit to cope
With that obstreperous joy success would bring,
I hardly tried now to rebuke the spring
My heart made, finding failure in its scope.

As when a sick man very near to death
Seems dead indeed, and feels begin and end
The tears and takes the farewell of each friend,
And hears one bid the other go, draw breath
Freelier outside, (``since all is o'er," he saith,
``And the blow fallen no grieving can amend;")

While some discuss if near the other graves
Be room enough for this, and when a day
Suits best for carrying the corpse away,
With care about the banners, scarves and staves:
And still the man hears all, and only craves
He may not shame such tender love and stay.

Thus, I had so long suffered in this quest,
Heard failure prophesied so oft, been writ
So many times among ``The Band"---to wit,
The knights who to the Dark Tower's search addressed
Their steps---that just to fail as they, seemed best,
And all the doubt was now---should I be fit?

So, quiet as despair, I turned from him,
That hateful cripple, out of his highway
Into the path he pointed. All the day
Had been a dreary one at best, and dim
Was settling to its close, yet shot one grim
Red leer to see the plain catch its estray.

For mark! no sooner was I fairly found
Pledged to the plain, after a pace or two,
Than, pausing to throw backward a last view
O'er the safe road, 'twas gone; grey plain all round:
Nothing but plain to the horizon's bound.
I might go on; nought else remained to do.

So, on I went. I think I never saw
Such starved ignoble nature; nothing throve:
For flowers---as well expect a cedar grove!
But cockle, spurge, according to their law
Might propagate their kind, with none to awe,
You'd think; a burr had been a treasure-trove.

No! penury, inertness and grimace,
In some strange sort, were the land's portion. ``See
``Or shut your eyes,'' said nature peevishly,
``It nothing skills: I cannot help my case:
``'Tis the Last judgment's fire must cure this place,
``Calcine its clods and set my prisoners free.''

If there pushed any ragged thistle-stalk
Above its mates, the head was chopped; the bents
Were jealous else. What made those holes and rents
In the dock's harsh swarth leaves, bruised as to baulk
All hope of greenness? 'tis a brute must walk
Pashing their life out, with a brute's intents.

As for the grass, it grew as scant as hair
In leprosy; thin dry blades pricked the mud
Which underneath looked kneaded up with blood.
One stiff blind horse, his every bone a-stare,
Stood stupefied, however he came there:
Thrust out past service from the devil's stud!

Alive? he might be dead for aught I know,
With that red gaunt and colloped neck a-strain,
And shut eyes underneath the rusty mane;
Seldom went such grotesqueness with such woe;
I never saw a brute I hated so;
He must be wicked to deserve such pain.

I shut my eyes and turned them on my heart.
As a man calls for wine before he fights,
I asked one draught of earlier, happier sights,
Ere fitly I could hope to play my part.
Think first, fight afterwards---the soldier's art:
One taste of the old time sets all to rights.

Not it! I fancied Cuthbert's reddening face
Beneath its garniture of curly gold,
Dear fellow, till I almost felt him fold
An arm in mine to fix me to the place,
That way he used. Alas, one night's disgrace!
Out went my heart's new fire and left it cold.

Giles then, the soul of honour---there he stands
Frank as ten years ago when knighted first.
What honest man should dare (he said) he durst.
Good---but the scene shifts---faugh! what hangman hands
Pin to his breast a parchment? His own bands
Read it. Poor traitor, spit upon and curst!

Better this present than a past like that;
Back therefore to my darkening path again!
No sound, no sight as far as eye could strain.
Will the night send a howlet or a bat?
I asked: when something on the dismal flat
Came to arrest my thoughts and change their train.

A sudden little river crossed my path
As unexpected as a serpent comes.
No sluggish tide congenial to the glooms;
This, as it frothed by, might have been a bath
For the fiend's glowing hoof---to see the wrath
Of its black eddy bespate with flakes and spumes.

So petty yet so spiteful! All along,
Low scrubby alders kneeled down over it;
Drenched willows flung them headlong in a fit
Of route despair, a suicidal throng:
The river which had done them all the wrong,
Whate'er that was, rolled by, deterred no whit.

Which, while I forded,---good saints, how I feared
To set my foot upon a dead man's cheek,
Each step, or feel the spear I thrust to seek
For hollows, tangled in his hair or beard!
---It may have been a water-rat I speared,
But, ugh! it sounded like a baby's shriek.

Glad was I when I reached the other bank.
Now for a better country. Vain presage!
Who were the strugglers, what war did they wage,
Whose savage trample thus could pad the dank
Soil to a plash? Toads in a poisoned tank,
Or wild cats in a red-hot iron cage---

The fight must so have seemed in that fell cirque.
What penned them there, with all the plain to choose?
No foot-print leading to that horrid mews,
None out of it. Mad brewage set to work
Their brains, no doubt, like galley-slaves the Turk
Pits for his pastime, Christians against Jews.

And more than that---a furlong on---why, there!
What bad use was that engine for, that wheel,
Or brake, not wheel---that harrow fit to reel
Men's bodies out like silk? with all the air
Of Tophet's tool, on earth left unaware,
Or brought to sharpen its rusty teeth of steel.

Then came a bit of stubbed ground, once a wood,
Next a marsh, it would seem, and now mere earth
Desperate and done with; (so a fool finds mirth,
Makes a thing and then mars it, till his mood
Changes and off he goes!) within a rood---
Bog, clay and rubble, sand and stark black dearth.

Now blotches rankling, coloured gay and grim,
Now patches where some leanness of the soil's
Broke into moss or substances like boils;
Then came some palsied oak, a cleft in him
Like a distorted mouth that splits its rim
Gaping at death, and dies while it recoils.

And just as far as ever from the end!
Nought in the distance but the evening, nought
To point my footstep further! At the thought,
great black bird, Apollyon's bosom-friend,
Sailed past, nor beat his wide wing dragon-penned
That brushed my cap---perchance the guide I sought.

For, looking up, aware I somehow grew,
'Spite of the dusk, the plain had given place
All round to mountains---with such name to grace
Mere ugly heights and heaps now stolen in view.
How thus they had surprised me,---solve it, you!
How to get from them was no clearer case.

Yet half I seemed to recognize some trick
Of mischief happened to me, God knows when---
In a bad dream perhaps. Here ended, then,
Progress this way. When, in the very nick
Of giving up, one time more, came a click
As when a trap shuts---you're inside the den!

Burningly it came on me all at once,
This was the place! those two hills on the right,
Crouched like two bulls locked horn in horn in fight;
While to the left, a tall scalped mountain ... Dunce,
Dotard, a-dozing at the very nonce,
After a life spent training for the sight!

What in the midst lay but the Tower itself?
The round squat turret, blind as the fool's heart,
Built of brown stone, without a counter-part
In the whole world. The tempest's mocking elf
Points to the shipman thus the unseen shelf
He strikes on, only when the timbers start.

*Not see? because of night perhaps?---why, day*
*Came back again for that! before it left,*
*The dying sunset kindled through a cleft:*
*The hills, like giants at a hunting, lay,*
*Chin upon hand, to see the game at bay,---*
*``Now stab and end the creature---to the heft!"*

*Not hear? when noise was everywhere! it tolled*
*Increasing like a bell. Names in my ears*
*Of all the lost adventurers my peers,---*
*How such a one was strong, and such was bold,*
*And such was fortunate, yet, each of old*
*Lost, lost! one moment knelled the woe of years.*

*There they stood, ranged along the hill-sides, met*
*To view the last of me, a living frame*
*For one more picture! in a sheet of flame*
*I saw them and I knew them all. And yet*
*Dauntless the slug-horn to my lips I set,*
*And blew."*

~~ Robert Browning

# Postscript

*"Because we had culture, we were never truly subjugated. Because we have culture, we will one day take back the spaces."*  ~~ Lauri Love

My first book *Behind The Mask: An Inside Look At Anonymous* encompassed a time period of approximately four years. *Dark Ops: An Anonymous Story* likewise takes in the next four year period in the story, which is still not finished yet. Of the eight years encompassed in these two books, I have spent six of them on the run from the FBI Cyber Crime Division. And five of those years have been spent here in Canada, in hiding and seeking sanctuary from the US government's pogrom against Information Activists. This is the story of my Resistance. This is the story of my life inside the *Global Collective of Anonymous*.

I chose the title "Dark Ops" because I knew that this book would be less about adventure and more about the actual *Anonymous Operations* I helped to launch during my exile from the USA in Canada. And because these next generation Anonymous Operations were so different, and so ominous, than what had come before - I decided to call them the "Dark Ops". I came to Canada with a threefold mission. First, to not get caught, and eventually find political asylum in a third country. Second, I wanted to continue the important work in the *Anonymous Global Collective* as it continued to evolve into one of the most potent socio-political movements in human history. Finally I had as a goal to eventually get these books to the world so that this remarkable story might be preserved for future Anons and history. Five years later, and the books are published and the FBI still has yet to "get its man". That leaves only my accounting for what I did within Information Activism and the *Anonymous Global Collective* while in exile. This is what *Dark Ops: An Anonymous Story* is. This is my account of what I did with the liberty I stole from a USA government determined to lock me up and shut me up.

Just as we saw in *Behind The Mask: An Inside Look At Anonymous*, this new cycle in the history of the Global Collective saw two new genres of

*Anonymous Operation* evolve - the *Justice Ops* and *Social Ops*. These now joined the original *Censorship Ops* and *Freedom Ops* to complete the range of global issues *Anonymous* can now effect. These two new genres are strangely binary, in the sense that *Justice Ops* primarily focus on a single victim of injustice (one thing that makes them so controversial within the Collective) whereas *Social Ops* are aimed at entire swaths of the global population. An excellent example is *Anonymous Operation Safe Winter*, in which thousands of Anons in hundreds of cities around the world fan out and provide substantial aid to homeless people in the winter months - and advocate for them online the rest of the year.

As I pen this Donald Trump has become President of the USA. And apparently someone better skilled than either us or the GOP hackers we encountered in Chapter One has hacked the DNC and possibly the vote counting systems in several battleground States. And strangely, I am as lost to predict the future of Anonymous now as I was at the end of *Behind The Mask: An Inside Look At Anonymous*. Just as Anonymous defies any attempt to define it, it likewise resists any efforts to predict what it will do and become next. And this is from someone on the *inside* actually working to create that future for the Global Collective. I can't imagine how confused the rest of the world must be when trying to figure out *Anonymous*.

As for my own future, I'm likewise completely in the dark. In writing these last few paragraphs, my own story, as well as the story of my involvement in *Anonymous* - is now up-to-date. I face the future now just like you, the reader - with no real idea what will happen next. I can tell you I remain as devoted as ever to this idea called *Anonymous*. I continue to engage in conversations with various nation states to attempt to acquire political asylum status. And I remain determined to remain in hiding here in Canada with the purpose of not being captured and silenced by the USA regime. All I can say to my readers, supporters, fans, and even my enemies is that I *will* continue to raise my voice against tyranny, and work hard to build up the *Anonymous Global Collective*.

www.CommanderX.info


Commander X - February 21, 2017 - North York, Ontario - Canada

# Acknowledgments

*"As we express our gratitude, we must never forget that the highest appreciation is not to utter words, but to live by them."* ~~ John F. Kennedy

I'd like to begin by simply repeating my deepest gratitude to everyone mentioned in my acknowledgments for *Behind The Mask: An Inside Look At Anonymous*. You are all as much responsible for my completion of this book as my last, which of course might not earn you any respect from some people who oppose my work - most especially the government of the USA and NATO. Nevertheless I remain deeply grateful to you all.

Since arriving in exile here in Canada, many Canadians, both Anons and supporters, have gone to great expense and effort, and put themselves and their families in harms way - to become my support network up here. Not only would this book not have been written without your assistance, but given the harsh environment up here I may well not even have survived without your support. Obviously I can't name you, but you have a special gratitude from me and special place in my heart forever. Thank you for the risks you took for me, the help you provided, the support you freely gave, and the love. The last is returned in full measure.

I would like to acknowledge and tip my hat to the many thousands of Friends, Anons, Hacktivists, supporters and fans who follow me on social media, in particular on *Twitter*. In the past five years of exile you have kept me continuously uplifted with your wit, concern, and loving support - all delivered in 140 character doses. You made me laugh when I was sad, you made me smile when I was angry, you made me brave when I was scared out of my wits. Most of you I don't even know personally. Some of you have become life-long friends. My Twitter Family is special to me. From you I gained many inspirations that made their way into *Dark Ops: An Anonymous Story,* but more importantly you made me a part of a community, when AFK I was completely and utterly alone. Thank you all.

A thank you is definitely due for both of my publishers, Lulu (print editions - www.lulu.com) and SmashWords (eBook editions - www.SmashWords.com) not only for their incredible self-publishing platforms and assistance getting these books to the people, but for protecting those works from the tyrannical authorities and others who would silence me. Both my publishers protected my books, and helped me get them ready and delivered to the world. I encourage anyone, but especially other hackers or Information Activists, to not be afraid to publish. While it's not easy, these publishers will give you the tools and advice you need for *free* to get your book to the world.

Finally, I would like to acknowledge the pain and sacrifice my Family has gone through in the past eight years, in particular my Sister Amy Beth and my Nephews Adam, Joshua and Richard. When the shit began to hit the fan for me and *Anonymous* back in 2009 I made a conscious decision to sever any communication, no matter how covert - with my Family. I did this to protect both them, from being used by the FBI against me - or vice versa. In spite of this, my little Sister Amy Beth in particular has become one of my most vocal supporters on social media. Neither of us is young, and it's quite possible it may never be safe to tell you in person while we're both alive. But I love you with all my heart Amy, and your support means more to me than anything in the world.

The quote at the head of these acknowledgments sums up precisely how I have approached my unending gratitude to everyone mentioned here and in my last book. All of you made sacrifices to help me continue my work as an Information Activist these past eight years. I have tried to repay and legitimize that sacrifice by working night and day to build up *Anonymous* and information activism, and to make the world a little bit more free and just. I have tried to spend wisely every moment of liberty you all have purchased for me with your support. And I will keep doing this until I am captured, killed, or die from the rigors of exile. I am not often very vocal about how much I appreciate each of you. I prefer to thank you by working to make what you all have given me mean something.

www.AnonymousGlobal.org

FERGUSON POLICE
JUST EXECUTED
MY UNARMED SON!!!

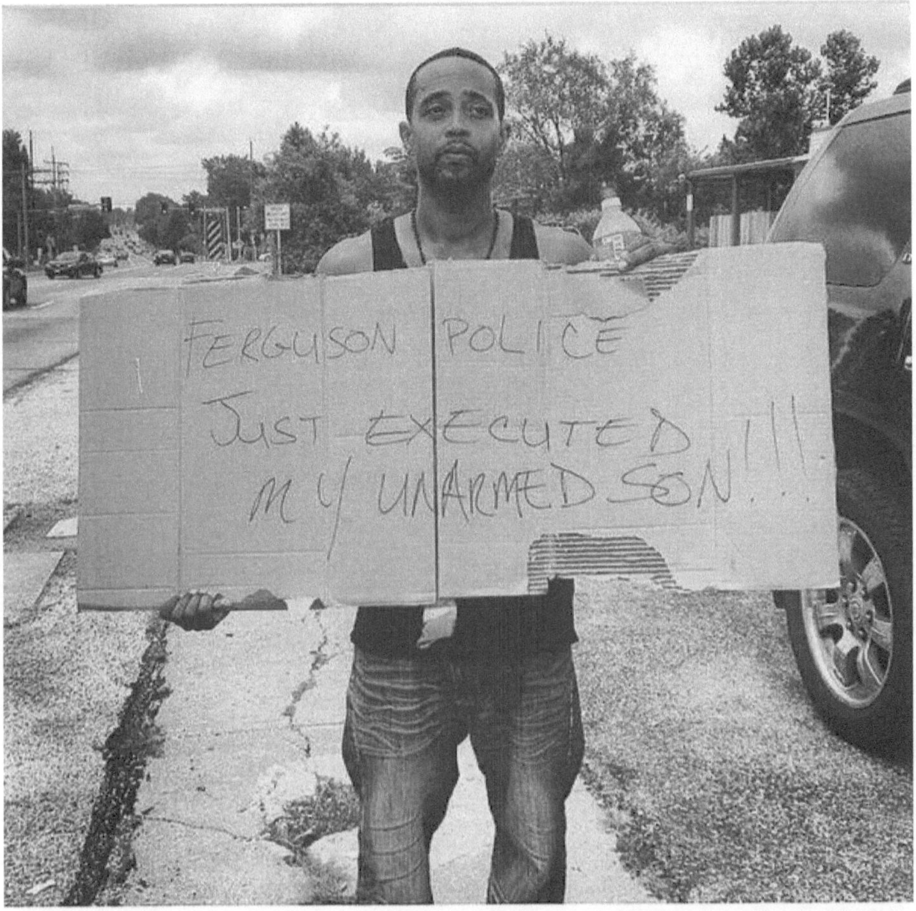

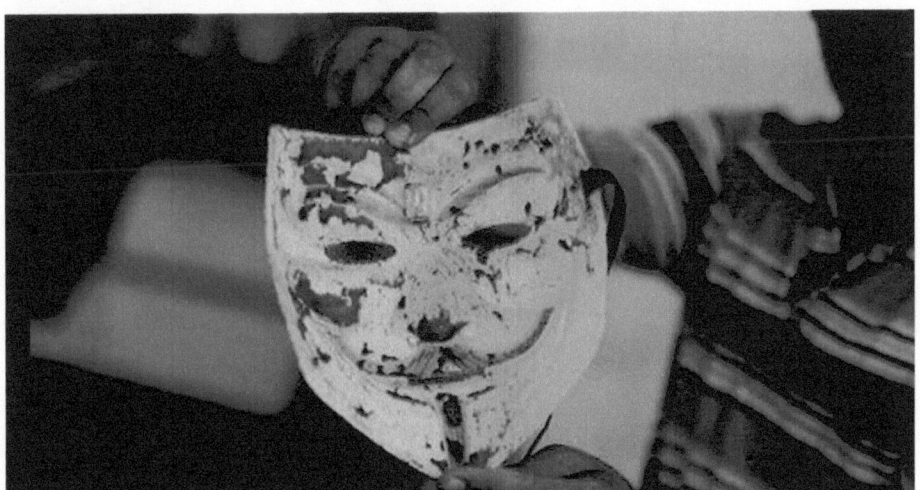

# References

For the convenience of my print readers, a hyperlinked version of these reference articles and media is located here:
http://commanderx.info/darkops/references.html

---------------------------

Anonymous reflects on a "frantic and historic" year -
http://www.salon.com/2012/12/27/anonymous_reflects_on_a_frantic_and_historic_year/

Did Anonymous Save the Election from Karl Rove?  (Part 1) -
https://www.youtube.com/watch?v=QITGHymqZvo

Did Anonymous Save the Election from Karl Rove?  (Part 2) -
https://www.youtube.com/watch?v=3J2NMyUncos

Anonymous Saved The Election?  -
http://www.addictinginfo.org/2012/11/17/anonymous-saved-the-election-text/

Did Anonymous stop Rove from stealing the election?  -
http://www.salon.com/2012/11/20/did_anonymous_stop_rove_stealing_the_election/

Anonymous, Karl Rove and 2012 Election Fix?  -
http://www.truth-out.org/news/item/12845-anonymous-karl-rove-and-2012-election-fix

Did Hacker Group Anonymous Stop Karl Rove from Hijacking Election?  -
http://www.opposingviews.com/i/politics/2012-election/did-hacker-group-anonymous-stop-karl-rove-hijacking-election

Nonprofit says letter from hacker group corroborates Anonymous video - http://dailycaller.com/2012/11/23/nonprofit-says-letter-from-hacker-group-corroborates-anonymous-video/

Anonymous warns Israel: 'No one cuts internet on our watch!' - https://www.rt.com/news/gaza-israel-strike-anonymous-787/

Anonymous launches #OpIsrael to support Gaza during attacks - http://www.dailydot.com/news/anonymous-opisrael-gaza-internet-access/

As Israel attacks Gaza, Palestinians find an unlikely ally - https://tribune.com.pk/story/466092/as-israel-attacks-gaza-palestinians-find-an-unlikely-ally/

Anonymous Hackers Hit Israeli Sites In Retaliation For Gaza Attacks - http://www.forbes.com/sites/andygreenberg/2012/11/15/anonymous-hackers-deface-israeli-sites-in-retaliation-for-gaza-attacks/

Anonymous Launches #OPIsrael in Response to Israel's Live-Tweeted Attack on Gaza - http://observer.com/2012/11/anonymous-launches-opisrael-in-response-to-israels-live-tweeted-attack-on-gaza-strip/

Anonymous Attacks Israeli Web Sites - https://bits.blogs.nytimes.com/2012/11/15/anonymous-attacks-israeli-web-sites/?_r=0

Anonymous Attacks Israeli Websites To Show Gaza Support In Conflict - http://www.huffingtonpost.com/2012/11/15/anonymous-israel-gaza_n_2139325.html

Anonymous retaliates to Israel's Gaza Internet threat - http://www.salon.com/2012/11/15/anonymous_retaliates_to_israels_gaza_internet_threat/

Anonymous Hackers Target Israel After Gaza Airstrike - http://www.foxbusiness.com/features/2012/11/15/anonymous-hackers-target-israel-after-gaza-airstrike.html

Anonymous targets Israeli sites, offers Gazans internet help - https://www.scmagazine.com/anonymous-targets-israeli-sites-offers-gazans-internet-help/article/543284/

Israeli, Hamas Conflict Attracts Anonymous - http://www.eweek.com/security/israeli-hamas-conflict-attracts-anonymous

Group Anonymous attacks Israeli websites to retaliate against bombing of Gaza - http://english.alarabiya.net/articles/2012/11/16/250005.html

Anonymous hacker group attacks Israeli websites - http://www.bbc.com/news/technology-20356757

Hacktivist group Anonymous rallies to Gaza's side with #OpIsrael offensive - https://www.infosecurity-magazine.com/news/hacktivist-group-anonymous-rallies-to-gazas-side/

Anonymous attacks Israeli websites in response to Gaza attacks - http://www.digitaljournal.com/article/337011

Anonymous attacks Israeli websites over Gaza bombings - http://www.theregister.co.uk/2012/11/16/anonymous_attacks_israel/

Anonymous targets Israeli websites in response to attacks in Gaza - http://venturebeat.com/2012/11/15/anonymous-idf/

Anonymous enters Israel-Hamas cyber war, takes down 40 Israeli sites - http://www.firstpost.com/world/anonymous-enters-israel-hamas-cyber-war-takes-down-40-israeli-sites-525839.html

Anonymous all out assault for #OpIsrael leaves sites hacked, defaced and leaked - https://www.cyberwarnews.info/2012/11/17/anonymous-all-out-assault-for-opisrael-leaves-sites-hacked-defaced-and-leaked/

Israeli Vice Prime Minister Twitter Account Hacked - https://www.copybook.com/news/israeli-vice-prime-minister-twitter-account-hacked

The Vice Prime Minister of Israel Was Just Hacked on Twitter and Facebook - http://gawker.com/5962371/the-israeli-vice-prime-minister-was-just-twitter-and-facebook-hacked

Pope's butler arrested over Vatican documents leak - http://www.cnn.com/2012/05/26/world/europe/italy-vatican-leak/

Anonymous Operation Vatican Video Release - https://vimeo.com/217848380

The Pope's butler arrested following Vatileaks investigation - http://www.telegraph.co.uk/news/worldnews/europe/vaticancityandholysee/9290768/The-Popes-butler-arrested-following-Vatileaks-investigation.html

Pope Benedict sends first personal tweet - http://www.cnn.com/2012/12/12/world/europe/vatican-pope-twitter/

Pope Benedict pardons former butler Paolo Gabriele - http://www.bbc.com/news/world-europe-20824814

Pope Benedict pardons his butler - http://www.telegraph.co.uk/news/worldnews/the-pope/9762692/Pope-Benedict-pardons-his-butler.html

Pope orders frees jailed Vatileaks priest -
http://www.news.com.au/world/breaking-news/pope-orders-frees-jailed-vatileaks-priest/news-story/f69e87fd4d3eb86fe61ce6b8c71fe97f

Inside the Anonymous Hacking File on the Steubenville 'Rape Crew' -
https://www.theatlantic.com/national/archive/2013/01/inside-anonymous-hacking-file-steubenville-rape-crew/317301/

Social media casts spotlight on Ohio rape case -
http://www.cnn.com/2013/01/03/justice/ohio-rape-online-video/index.html

FBI Gets Involved in Case; Second Occupy Steubenville Bigger Than First -
http://www.yourohiovalley.com/story/20487742/new-video-released-on-steubenville-rape-authorities-release-statement

Anonymous Leaks Video Of Football Players Making Fun Of Rape Victim -
http://www.webpronews.com/anonymous-leaks-video-of-football-players-making-fun-of-rape-victim-2013-01/

Steubenville High school students joke about rape in video leaked by Anonymous - http://scallywagandvagabond.com/2013/01/steubenville-high-school-students-joke-about-rape-in-video-leaked-by-anonymous/

Anonymous Hackers leaks video of Steubenville rape case -
http://thehackernews.com/2013/01/anonymous-hackers-leaks-video-of.html

Hackers produce disturbing video evidence in Ohio gang rape case -
http://www.rawstory.com/2013/01/hackers-produce-disturbing-video-evidence-in-ohio-gang-rape-case/

The controversial, Anonymous-leaked video of Steubenville High School athletes mocking a rape victim -
http://theweek.com/article/index/238386/the-controversial-anonymous-leaked-video-of-steubenville-high-school-athletes-mocking-a-rape-victim

LocalLeaks Charges Cover-Up by Parents, Police in Steubenville Rape Forces Official Response - https://www.opednews.com/populum/page.php?f=LocalLeaks-Explosive-Repo-by-Gustav-Wynn-130104-862.html

Anonymous turns private eye in Ohio rape case - http://www.theregister.co.uk/2013/01/04/anonymous_ohio_rape_case/

Steubenville High school rape case leads to new Anonymous leaks & new names - http://scallywagandvagabond.com/2013/01/steubenville-high-school-rape-case-leads-to-new-anonymous-leaks-new-names/

Local Leaks Tipsters Allege Steubenville Victim Was Drugged - https://www.theatlantic.com/national/archive/2013/01/local-leaks-tipsters-allege-steubenville-victim-was-drugged/319733/

How Anonymous Hacking Exposed Steubenville High School Rape Case - http://www.alternet.org/how-anonymous-hacking-exposed-steubenville-high-school-rape-case?page=0%2C0

Anonymous Releases More Intel on the Alleged Steubenville 'Rape Crew' - http://jezebel.com/5973165/anonymous-releases-more-intel-on-the-alleged-steubenville-rape-crew

Hacker Group Anonymous Leaks Chilling Video in Case of Alleged Steubenville Rape, Cover-Up - https://www.democracynow.org/2013/1/7/hacker_group_anonymous_leaks_chilling_video

Rape In Steubenville Attracts Anonymous' Attention To Injustice And Corruption On Main Street, USA - http://legalschnauzer.blogspot.jp/2013/01/rape-in-steubenville-attracts-anonymous.html

Why Nobody Trusts Steubenville - https://www.yahoo.com/news/why-nobody-trusts-steubenville-171732708.html

The Steubenville Gang Rape: A Timeline - http://www.dailykos.com/story/2013/01/03/1176096/-The-Steubenville-Gang-Rape-A-Timeline#

Steubenville Rape Case Splits Town Between Big Red and Guy Fawkes - http://www.thedailybeast.com/articles/2013/01/07/steubenville-rape-case-splits-town-between-big-red-and-guy-fawkes

Authorities In Steubenville Rape Case Launch Website To Refute Claims From Anonymous Hackers, Media - http://www.ibtimes.com/authorities-steubenville-rape-case-launch-website-refute-claims-anonymous-hackers-media-995662

A Conversation With Anonymous - http://www.huffingtonpost.com/michealene-cristini-risley/a-conversation-with-anony_b_2433813.html

Inside the Search for the Truth About Steubenville — 1,000 Tips at a Time - https://www.theatlantic.com/national/archive/2013/01/local-leaks-steubenville-files/319729/

The Steubenville 'Rape Crew' Trial Will Be on Display for the World to See - https://www.theatlantic.com/national/archive/2013/01/steubenville-trial-news/318857/

Whither whistleblowing: Where have all the leaking sites gone? - https://arstechnica.com/business/2013/03/whither-whistleblowing-where-have-all-the-leaking-sites-gone/

Anonymous protests outside Ohio court as rape trial begins - https://www.rt.com/usa/anonymous-stebenville-rape-trial-226/

Enter the Trial in Steubenville, Where the Cast Is Not Merely Football Players - https://www.theatlantic.com/national/archive/2013/03/steubenville-rape-trial-players/317443/

Requiem for a Dream - http://www.newyorker.com/magazine/2013/03/11/requiem-for-a-dream

Aaron Swartz stood up for freedom and fairness – and was hounded to his death - https://www.theguardian.com/commentisfree/2015/feb/07/aaron-swartz-suicide-internets-own-boy

The Brilliant Life and Tragic Death of Aaron Swartz - http://www.rollingstone.com/culture/news/the-brilliant-life-and-tragic-death-of-aaron-swartz-20130215

Tribute To Jane Doe: You Will Never Be Alone OpRollRedRoll - https://www.youtube.com/watch?v=iJBzErisdIo

Operation Bahrain Anonymous Press Release - http://thehackernews.com/2011/02/operation-bahrain-opbahrain-anonymous.html

Anonymous to strike as Bahrain backs jail sentences for king insults - https://www.rt.com/news/bahrain-insults-f1-anonymous-882/

Anonymous Operation Bahrain Press Release - https://www.anonymous-france.eu/anonymous-operation-bahrain-press-release.html

Anonymous Operation Bahrain: Video Release - https://vimeo.com/64127103

Anonymous Operation Bahrain: Tamarrod Bahrain Action - https://www.indybay.org/newsitems/2013/08/14/18741546.phphttps://www.indybay.org/newsitems/2013/08/14/18741546.php

Anonymous #OpBahrain starts, will attack various websites of the regime - http://www.hackersnewsbulletin.com/2013/08/anonymous-opbahrain-starts-will-attack-various-websites-of-the-regime.html

Why didn't CNN's international arm air its own documentary on Bahrain's Arab Spring repression? - https://www.theguardian.com/world/2012/sep/04/cnn-international-documentary-bahrain-arab-spring-repression

The Clouds of Death - https://www.youtube.com/watch?v=_blU8no1fBo

Project PM Investigation of Qorvis - http://wiki.project-pm.org/wiki/Qorvis

Anonymous, Türkiye'deki devlet sitelerine saldırıya başladı! - http://webrazzi.com/2013/06/02/anonymous-opturkey/

Anonymous declares Op Turkey, attacks govt websites in support of protests - https://www.rt.com/news/anonymous-internet-turkey-protest-140/

Anonymous launches attacks against Turkish government for Gezi Park protests - http://www.hurriyetdailynews.com/anonymous-launches-attacks-against-turkish-government-for-gezi-park-protests.aspx?pageID=238&nID=48089&NewsCatID=359

Anonymous 'hacktivists' attack Turkish govt. sites amid protests - http://www.panarmenian.net/eng/news/160697/Anonymous_'hacktivists_attack_Turkish_govt_sites_amid_protests

Global "hacktivist" group launches attack on Turkish govt - http://www.worldbulletin.net/?aType=haber&ArticleID=110413

Hackers Attack Turkish Govt. Sites in Support of Protests - https://sputniknews.com/world/20130603181477150-Hackers-Attack-Turkish-Govt-Sites-in-Support-of-Protests/

Op Turkey: Anonymous Hacks 145 Turkish Websites And Shares Free Internet Access To Protestors In Turkey - http://www.ibtimes.com/opturkey-anonymous-hacks-145-turkish-websites-shares-free-internet-access-protestors-turkey-1290799

Anonymous, Syrian Electronic Army Reportedly Attack Turkish Government Websites - http://www.huffingtonpost.com/2013/06/05/anonymous-syrian-electronic-army_n_3390466.html

Anonymous, Syrian Electronic Army hack Turkish govt networks, leak emails incl PM's - https://www.rt.com/news/anonymous-turkey-emails-government-252/

Anonymous hacks Turkish Prime Minister website - http://www.hurriyetdailynews.com/anonymous-hacks-turkish-pm-website-claim.aspx?pageID=238&nID=48246&NewsCatID=341

Anonymous hacks TV watchdog for fining live streaming of Gezi protests - http://www.hurriyetdailynews.com/anonymous-hacks-tv-watchdog-for-fining-live-streaming-of-gezi-protests.aspx?pageID=238&nID=48718&NewsCatID=341

RedHack and Anonymous Team Up for November 5 Protests - http://news.softpedia.com/news/RedHack-and-Anonymous-Team-Up-for-November-5-Protests-392990.shtml

Terrorist organization? Turkish hackers face quarter-century prison terms -
https://www.rt.com/news/redhack-turkey-terrorism-trial-056/

Hackers RedHack Leak Details of Hundreds of Turkish Government Officials - http://www.ibtimes.co.uk/hackers-redhack-leak-details-hundreds-turkish-government-officials-1435008

Turkish Hackers Say They Deleted $670 Billion In Electricity Bills - http://www.mintpressnews.com/turkish-hackers-say-they-deleted-670-billion-in-electricity-bills/198955/

RedHack Hacks Website of Soma Municipality Following Death of Hundreds of Miners -
http://news.softpedia.com/news/RedHack-Hacks-Website-of-Soma-Municipality-Following-Death-of-Hundreds-of-Miners-442076.shtml

Hacked emails: Erdogan's son-in-law imported ISIS oil -
http://www.wnd.com/2016/12/hacked-emails-erdogans-son-in-law-imported-isis-oil/

Why RedHack challenges Turkey's political establishment -
https://www.dailydot.com/layer8/redhack-interview-turkey-censorship/

RedHack Hacks Turkish police website as border traffic grounds to a halt -
http://www.hurriyetdailynews.com/redhack-hacks-turkish-police-website-as-border-traffic-grounds-to-a-halt.aspx?pageID=238&nID=53904&NewsCatID=341

An Evening Of Resistance: A Conversation With Commander X, Tef Poe and Bassem Masri -
https://www.anonymous-france.eu/anon-uk-radio-operation-ferguson.html

Protests Over Michael Brown's Death Turn Chaotic, Anonymous & Benjamin Crump Join Cause - https://globalgrind.cassiuslife.com/4003307/michael-browns-death-protests-chaotic-anonymous-benjamin-crump-join-cause-video/

Anonymous Hits Back at Ferguson Police with Op Ferguson - https://thecryptosphere.com/2014/08/11/anonymous-hits-back-at-ferguson-police-with-opferguson/

Anonymous Vows Action Over Shooting Death of Unarmed Teen - http://gawker.com/anonymous-vows-action-over-shooting-death-of-unarmed-te-1619233440?utm_campaign=socialflow_gawker_facebook&utm_source=gawker_facebook&utm_medium=socialflow

Anonymous Launches "Operation Ferguson" For Mike Brown, The Missouri Teen Shot By Cops - https://www.bustle.com/articles/35237-anonymous-launches-operation-ferguson-for-mike-brown-the-missouri-teen-shot-by-cops

Anonymous 'hacktivists' get into city of Ferguson's websites Sunday night - http://www.upi.com/Top_News/US/2014/08/11/Anonymous-hacktivists-get-into-city-of-Fergusons-websites-Sunday-night/4231407771545/#ixzz3A6bjV75a

Anonymous launches Op Ferguson after cop kills unarmed Missouri teen - https://www.rt.com/usa/179532-anonymous-op-ferguson-missouri/

Anonymous takes action to protest police shooting of unarmed teen - http://www.deathandtaxesmag.com/226209/anonymous-takes-action-to-protest-police-shooting-of-unarmed-teen/

Op Ferguson Speaks! An exclusive interview - https://thecryptosphere.com/2014/08/11/opferguson-speaks-an-exclusive-interview/

Anonymous to conduct cyber attack on Ferguson PD for shooting unarmed teen - https://www.hackread.com/anonymous-cyber-attack-opferguson/

It's Back to Basics for Anonymous With Their Michael Brown Op - http://blackbag.gawker.com/its-back-to-basics-for-anonymous-with-their-michael-bro-1620177547

Big Brother, Little Sister: Op Ferguson in Images - https://thecryptosphere.com/2014/08/12/big-brother-little-sister-opferguson-in-images/

'Anonymous' launches operation against Mo. PD, hacks website - https://www.policeone.com/officer-shootings/articles/7456111-Anonymous-launches-operation-against-Mo-PD-hacks-website/

Anonymous' "Op Ferguson" Says It Will ID the Officer Who Killed Michael Brown - http://www.motherjones.com/politics/2014/08/anonymous-ferguson-police-killing-unarmed-michael-brown/

How computer hackers changed the Ferguson protests - http://www.stltoday.com/news/local/crime-and-courts/how-computer-hackers-changed-the-ferguson-protests/article_d81a1da4-ae04-5261-9064-e4c255111c94.html

BREAKING: Hacktavist Group Anonymous Releases Dispatch Tapes After Michael Brown Shooting - http://archives.bluenationreview.com/breaking-hacktavist-group-anonymous-releases-dispatch-tapes-michael-brown-shooting/

Anonymous plans to release name of cop who killed Michael Brown - https://www.dailydot.com/layer8/anonymous-ferguson-michael-brown-shooting-officer-name/

Anonymous Releases Alleged Police Dispatch Audio From Ferguson Shooting - http://mashable.com/2014/08/13/anonymous-st-louis-police-tapes-mike-brown/?utm_cid=mash-com-Tw-main-link#ABfzcNdINPqT

Op Ferguson Updates: Trolls, Honeypots, Leaks, and Crowdsourcing Intel - https://thecryptosphere.com/2014/08/13/opferguson-updates-trolls-honeypots-leaks-and-crowdsourcing-intel/

Anonymous hacks Ferguson, Mo., police site for dispatch tapes - https://www.cnet.com/news/anonymous-hacks-into-ferguson-police-site-for-dispatch-tapes/

How Anonymous Hackers Changed Ferguson, Mo., Protests - http://www.govtech.com/local/How-computer-hackers-changed-the-Ferguson-protests.html

Police suspect hackers shut down St. Louis County government websites - http://www.stltoday.com/news/local/crime-and-courts/st-louis-county-government-websites-are-down/article_b45783bf-572c-57b9-96dc-f7601d570c23.html

A Message From The #Ferguson Protesters To #Anonymous - https://thecryptosphere.com/2014/08/15/a-message-from-the-ferguson-protesters-to-anonymous/

Understanding Hacker Collective Anonymous & Operation Ferguson
http://www.bostonglobe.com/news/nation/2014/08/15/understanding-hacker-collective-anonymous-and-operation-ferguson/6gygWrRbYNJ4LNpAT4i5jN/story.html

Hackers have the names and Social Security numbers of Ferguson police. But should they share them? -
https://www.washingtonpost.com/news/the-intersect/wp/2014/08/14/hackers-have-the-names-and-social-security-numbers-of-ferguson-police-but-should-they-share-them/?utm_term=.8025902ab75e

Anonymous To ID Michael Brown's Killer – Already Has Paralyzed Ferguson -
http://addictinginfo.com/2014/08/14/anonymous-ferguson/

Locals Show Support For Operation Ferguson Outside Hattiesburg Police Department -
http://whlt.com/2014/08/17/locals-show-support-for-operation-ferguson-outside-hattiesburg-police-department/

Anonymous Targets Ferguson, Missouri in Op Ferguson; DDoS Attack on Local PD Web Site -
https://hotforsecurity.bitdefender.com/blog/anonymous-targets-ferguson-missouri-in-opferguson-ddos-attack-on-local-pd-web-site-9949.html

The Return of UGNazi: Doxing the Governor of Missouri -
https://thecryptosphere.com/2014/08/20/the-return-of-ugnazi-doxing-the-governor-of-missouri/

Op Ferguson and UGNazi in conversation: exclusive interviews -
https://thecryptosphere.com/2014/08/21/opferguson-and-ugnazi-in-conversation-exclusive-interviews/

What Anonymous Is Doing in Ferguson -
http://time.com/3148925/ferguson-michael-brown-anonymous/

HandsUpWalkOut: Anonymous and Op Ferguson call for General
Strike in Missouri -
https://thecryptosphere.com/2014/08/28/handsupwalkout-anonymous-
and-opferguson-call-for-general-strike-in-missouri/

Michael Brown Grand Jury Leaks: No Indictment Of Darren Wilson
Anonymous Claims -
http://www.inquisitr.com/1570675/michael-brown-grand-jury-leaks-
no-indictment-of-darren-wilson-anonymous-claims/

Anonymous Claims Ferguson Police Officer Darren Wilson Will Not
be Indicted for Mike Brown Killing -
http://www.ibtimes.co.uk/anonymous-claims-ferguson-police-officer-
darren-wilson-will-not-be-indicted-mike-brown-killing-1471910

Anonymous Unveils Explosive 'Leaks' on Michael Brown Grand Jury
and Ferguson Officer Darren Wilson -
http://www.theblaze.com/stories/2014/10/28/anonymous-unveils-
explosive-leaks-on-michael-brown-grand-jury-and-ferguson-officer-
darren-wilson-report/

Anonymous Leaks Darren Wilson Grand Jury Information; Claims To
Identify Alias -
http://www.business2community.com/us-news/anonymous-leaks-
darren-wilson-grand-jury-information-claims-identify-alias-
01051655#REDqAys6rKbPStgU.99

Anonymous Says Darren Wilson Will Go Free In Michael Brown
Death & Police On Alert For Riots -
http://www.inquisitr.com/1572114/leak-investigation-anonymous-
twitter-account-says-darren-wilson-will-go-free-in-michael-brown-
death-police-on-alert-for-riots/

Ferguson update: hacktivism, smear campaigns and missed court dates -
http://www.upi.com/Top_News/US/2014/10/28/Ferguson-update-hacktivism-smear-campaigns-and-missed-court-dates/6471414501079/?spt=nil_s&d=p

Anonymous: How hackers wreaked havoc in St. Louis -
http://www.stltoday.com/news/local/crime-and-courts/article_809a5d53-7d67-57ff-96f9-ee5772b395d0.html

Ferguson Grand Jury Decision: Darren Wilson -
http://www.inquisitr.com/1600376/ferguson-grand-jury-decision-darren-wilson/

The Battle of Ferguson II: Anonymous faces off with Klan in Op KKK -
http://theantimedia.org/anonymous-faces-off-with-klan-in-opkkk/

Anonymous Takes The Hoods Off The KKK After Threats Of 'Lethal Force' On Ferguson Protesters -
http://www.alan.com/2014/11/15/anonymous-takes-the-hoods-off-the-kkk-after-threats-of-lethal-force-on-ferguson-protesters/

Anonymous Reveals Photos, Names Of St. Louis Klansmen After Threats On Ferguson Protesters -
http://www.liberalamerica.org/2014/11/15/anonymous-kkk-ferguson/

Anonymous Unmasks Racist KKK Creeps Threatening Lethal Force Against Ferguson Protesters -
http://aattp.org/anonymous-unmasks-racist-kkk-creeps-threatening-lethal-force-against-ferguson-protectors-imagesvideo/

Anonymous Takes The Hoods Off KKK Members After Violent
Threats -
http://addictinginfo.com/2014/11/15/anonymous-expose-kkk/

Ferguson: Anonymous Reveals KKK Members Identities -
http://www.inquisitr.com/1612812/ferguson-anonymous-reveals-kkk-
members-identities/

Anonymous seizes Ku Klux Klan Twitter account over Ferguson
threats -
http://theantimedia.org/anonymous-faces-off-with-klan-in-opkkk/

Hacker group Anonymous publishes names of Ferguson KKK
members -
http://www.upi.com/Top_News/US/2014/11/16/Hacker-group-
Anonymous-publishes-names-of-Ferguson-KKK-
members/9011416181999/?spt=su

Anonymous hacks Ku Klux Klan twitter over Ferguson threats -
https://www.hackread.com/anonymous-hacks-kkk-twitter-over-
ferguson-threats/

Anonymous responds to KKK's twitter taunts by hacking, taking over
their account -
http://www.rawstory.com/2014/11/anonymous-responds-to-kkks-
twitter-taunts-by-hacking-taking-over-their-account/

OpKKK: Anonymous hacks KKK websites, Twitter over Ferguson
threats -
https://www.rt.com/usa/206067-anonymous-hacks-kkk-accounts/

Anonymous Exposes Cop as Member of KKK Behind Letter
Threatening to Kill Ferguson Protesters -
http://filmingcops.com/anonymous-exposes-cop-as-member-of-kkk-
behind-letter-threatening-to-kill-ferguson-protesters/

Ku Klux Klan Twitter accounts hacked by Anonymous over Ferguson threats -
http://www.independent.co.uk/news/world/americas/ku-klux-klan-twitter-accounts-hacked-by-anonymous-over-ferguson-threats-9864764.html

Anonymous Hacks Ku Klux Klan Twitter Accounts and Websites Following Ferguson Threats -
http://www.ibtimes.co.uk/anonymous-hacks-ku-klux-klan-twitter-accounts-websites-following-ferguson-threats-1475127?utm_source=dlvr.it&utm_medium=social&utm_campaign=ibtimesuk

Anonymous Is Going To War With The KKK Over Ferguson Protests
http://www.huffingtonpost.com/2014/11/17/anonymous-kkk_n_6173332.html

Hacker Group Anonymous Hacks KKK Accounts, Shows Members Faces -
http://www.theepochtimes.com/n3/1086152-hacker-group-anonymous-hacks-kkk-accounts-shows-members-faces/

Hacker-activist group Anonymous seizes KKK Twitter accounts; reveals identities -
http://fox2now.com/2014/11/17/hacker-activist-group-anonymous-seizes-kkk-twitter-accounts-reveals-identities/

Russia Beaming Ferguson & Anonymous News Into USA -
http://www.ksdk.com/news/local/russia-beaming-ferguson-and-anonymous-news-into-usa/278773085

'Let the war begin': Anonymous knocks hate sites offline as KKK 'hoods off' campaign continues -
http://www.rawstory.com/2014/11/let-the-war-begin-anonymous-knocks-hate-sites-offline-as-kkk-hoods-off-campaign-continues/#.VGt8WCbhUhw.twitter

KKK hit by cyberattack after Ferguson threats -
https://www.usatoday.com/story/news/nation-now/2014/11/18/anonymous-hacks-kkk-twitter-accounts-ferguson-threats/19215047/

Anonymous Leaks Map Of Federal Perimeter Around Ferguson - KKK Leader Exposed As Federal Agent -
https://www.infowars.com/anonymous-leaks-map-of-federal-perimeter-around-ferguson/

Anonymous takes over Ku Klux Klan's Twitter account -
https://www.theguardian.com/technology/2014/nov/17/anonymous-takes-over-ku-klux-klans-twitter-account?CMP=share_btn_tw

Anonymous Responds To KKK's 'Lethal Force' Ferguson Threat By Hacking Twitter Account -
http://www.politicususa.com/2014/11/17/anonymous-responds-kkks-lethal-force-ferguson-threat-hacking-twitter-account.html

Anonymous hacks the Ku Klux Klan after Ferguson threats -
http://www.theregister.co.uk/2014/11/18/anonymous_oppkkk/

Anonymous Hacks KKK After Group Threatens Ferguson Protesters -
http://www.christiantimes.com/article/anonymous-hacks-kkk-after-group-threatens-ferguson-protesters/49496.htm

Hacker Group Anonymous Takes Over Ku Klux Klan Twitter Account After Ferguson Threats -
http://www.techtimes.com/articles/20409/20141117/anonymous-attacks-kkk-ferguson-threats.htm

Anonymous Hacks & Seizes KKK Twitter Accounts -
https://www.freespeech.org/video/anonymous-hacks-seizes-kkk-twitter-accounts

What everyone gets wrong about violence in Ferguson -
https://www.dailydot.com/layer8/ferguson-protest-grand-jury-kkk-anonymous-media-militia-nixon/?tw=pl

Anonymous Seizes Ku Klux Klan Twitter Account Over Ferguson T`hreats -
https://popularresistance.org/anonymous-seizes-ku-klux-klan-twitter-account-over-ferguson-threats/

Anonymous takes on the Ku Klux Klan -
http://www.bbc.com/news/blogs-trending-30105412?ocid=socialflow_twitter

After Ferguson threat, Anonymous removes the KKK's hoods. Effective? -
http://www.csmonitor.com/USA/2014/1119/After-Ferguson-threat-Anonymous-removes-the-KKK-s-hoods.-Effective-video

Activist group Anonymous hacks KKK Twitter account -
http://www.scpr.org/news/2014/11/18/48162/activist-group-anonymous-hacks-kkk-twitter-account/

Anonymous Hackers unmask KKK members -
http://sportact.net/anonymous-hackers-unmask-kkk-members-4184-2014/

KKK hit by cyberattack after Ferguson threats -
http://www.indystar.com/story/news/nation/2014/11/18/anonymous-hacks-kkk-twitter-accounts-ferguson-threats-against-protesters/19226339/

Anonymous hacks Klu Klux Klan Twitter account in response to taunts -
http://metro.co.uk/2014/11/18/anonymous-hacks-klu-klux-klan-twitter-account-in-response-to-taunts-4953450/

Anonymous: Ferguson Killer Cop Darren Wilson 'Linked to KKK Ghoul Squad' -
http://www.ibtimes.co.uk/anonymous-ferguson-killer-cop-darren-wilson-linked-kkk-ghoul-squad-1475953

A cause for Internet hacking: Anonymous vs KKK -
http://www.thedaonline.com/opinion/article_57d3905e-713e-11e4-b522-43f048696e20.html

Ferguson: Anonymous Vows To Release Evidence Linking Darren Wilson To The KKK -
http://www.inquisitr.com/1623199/ferguson-anonymous-vows-to-release-evidence-linking-darren-wilson-to-the-kkk/#utm_content=buffer897f0&utm_medium=social&utm_source=twitter.com&utm_campaign=buffer

Ferguson KKK Threat: Anonymous Mask Wearing N****r Lovers Will Be 'Strung Up Next To Chimps' -
http://www.inquisitr.com/1625053/ferguson-kkk-threat-anonymous-mask-wearing-nr-lovers-will-be-strung-up-next-to-chimps/

The Traditionalist American Knights Of The KKK Want to Kill The Group Anonymous -
http://www.politicusa.com/2014/11/22/traditionalist-american-knights-kkk-kill-group-anonymous.html

Anonymous Posts Credit Card Details of KKK Grand Wizard who Threatened 'Lethal Force' in Ferguson -
http://www.ibtimes.co.uk/anonymous-publishes-credit-card-details-kkk-grand-wizard-who-threatened-ferguson-protesters-1476931

Anonymous posts KKK leader's personal data online in ongoing war over Ferguson -
https://www.rt.com/usa/209875-anonymous-kkk-leader-dox/

Ferguson protesters clash with police across US - http://www.news.com.au/world/ferguson-protesters-clash-with-police-across-us/news-story/4c56ae778ae2686b447bd39b6f9f0778

Anonymous Publishes Purported Address, Credit Cards of Missouri KKK Leader - http://www.mediaite.com/online/anonymous-publishes-purported-address-credit-cards-of-missouri-kkk-leader/

Anonymous Hackers Dox Missouri KKK Leader — Release Phone, Credit Card Numbers, More - http://www.business2community.com/tech-gadgets/anonymous-hackers-dox-missouri-kkk-leader-release-phone-credit-card-numbers-01080384

Anonymous Declares Vengeance For Mike Brown: 'We Are The Law Now - http://www.inquisitr.com/1644481/anonymous-declares-vengeance-for-mike-brown-we-are-the-law-now/

Cyber Monday: Anonymous Calls For Boycott Of Sales & Attacks On Retailers In Ferguson Protest - http://www.independent.co.uk/life-style/gadgets-and-tech/news/cyber-monday-anonymous-calls-for-boycott-of-sales-and-attacks-on-retailers-in-ferguson-protest-9895001.html

The War Between the KKK and Anonymous - http://www.topsecretwriters.com/2014/12/war-kkk-anonymous/

The Signs & Symbols Of A Ferguson Folk Saint - http://www.frontpagemag.com/fpm/246732/signs-symbols-ferguson-folk-saint-dawn-perlmutter

Anonymous Threatens To Shut Down Iggy Azalea's USC Concert - http://www.thewrap.com/anonymous-threatens-to-shut-down-iggy-azaleas-usc-concert/

Anonymous brings down Oakland PD website after cops gas protesters - https://www.rt.com/usa/212335-police-protesters-oakland-gas/

Anonymous says it took down Oakland police, city websites - http://www.latimes.com/local/lanow/la-me-ln-anonymous-oakland-police-city-websites-20141210-story.html

Anonymous Takes Down Oakland Police Website & Twitter After Protester Shot - http://www.inquisitr.com/1668595/anonymous-takes-down-oakland-police-website-twitter-after-protester-shot-with-non-lethal-rounds/

Anonymous Targets Oakland City & Police Sites - http://www.newsweek.com/anonymous-targets-oakland-city-and-police-sites-290955

Anonymous Claims To Have Released The Officers Names Who Killed Kajieme Powell - http://thesource.com/2014/12/10/anonymous-claims-to-have-released-the-officers-names-who-killed-kajieme-powell/

Oakland City and Police Sites Down, Anonymous Hackers Claim Credit - http://www.ndtv.com/world-news/oakland-city-and-police-sites-down-anonymous-hackers-claim-credit-711407

Anonymous Is Targeting Brian Encinia & Plans A Day of Rage For Waller County Sheriff's Department - https://www.bustle.com/articles/101412-anonymous-is-targeting-brian-encinia-plans-a-day-of-rage-for-waller-county-sheriffs-department

Hackers Claim To Target Waller County Officials - http://www.click2houston.com/news/hackers-claim-to-target-waller-county-officials

Focus On KKK Ignores More Powerful Hate Groups - http://america.aljazeera.com/articles/2015/11/6/focus-on-kkk-ignores-otherl-white-hate-groups.html

Anonymous release identities of 1,000 alleged KKK members to mark first anniversary of Ferguson protests - http://www.dailymail.co.uk/news/article-3306394/Violent-bigotry-problem-United-States-Anonymous-release-identities-1-000-alleged-Ku-Klux-Klan-members-mark-anniversary-Ferguson-protests.html

Operation KKK Leaks: Will Anonymous Yank KKK Hoods Off Politicians, Cops Or Feds? - http://www.computerworld.com/article/3000372/cybercrime-hacking/operation-kkk-leaks-will-anonymous-yank-kkk-hoods-off-of-politicians-cops-feds.html

Overnight Cybersecurity: Anonymous begins outing alleged KKK members - http://thehill.com/policy/cybersecurity/overnight/258898-overnight-cybersecurity-anonymous-begins-unmasking-alleged-kkk-members

Anonymous Leaks Identities Of 350 Alleged Ku Klux Klan Members https://www.theguardian.com/technology/2015/nov/06/anonymous-ku-klux-klan-name-leak

The hacker group Anonymous has exposed hundreds of alleged Ku
Klux Klan members -
http://www.thejournal.ie/anonymous-operation-kkk-november-5-
2429072-Nov2015/

Anonymous Posts A List Containing Alleged Ku Klux Klan
Sympathisers -
http://us.blastingnews.com/news/2015/11/anonymous-posts-a-list-
containing-alleged-ku-klux-klan-sympathisers-00642569.html

KKK Targeted By Anonymous Hacktivism -
http://www.brockpress.com/2015/11/kkk-targeted-by-anonymous-
hacktivism/

Anonymous Gives A Clue To Who's In The Klan -
http://www.thestylus.net/news/view.php/1014342/Anonymous-gives-
a-clue-to-whos-in-the-Kl

A Hacker Attacked The Largest US Police Union & The Leaks Are
Just Beginning -
https://www.yahoo.com/news/hacker-attacked-largest-us-police-
204000991.html

Hacker Doxes 80 Police Officers Of Miami -
http://www.spamfighter.com/News-20080-Hacker-Doxes-80-Police-
Officers-of-Miami.htm

Hackers Target USA's Largest Police Union -
https://foreignpolicy.com/2016/01/29/hackers-target-americas-largest-
police-union/

Hacker Claims Breaching FBI Server, Exposes Details of 80 Miami
Police Officers -
https://www.hackread.com/fbi-server-hacked-miami-police-data-
leaked/

Infamous Hackers Targeting Mesa Police -
http://www.abc15.com/news/region-southeast-valley/mesa/infamous-hackers-targeting-mesa-officers-group-criticizing-officer-involved-shootings-

Hacker group warns Mesa PD -
http://www.eastvalleytribune.com/local/mesa/article_140d8180-d70a-11e5-b74c-57ff4384bf07.html

Widow Of Man Shot By Mesa Police Seeks Help From Anonymous -
http://www.tucsonnewsnow.com/story/31268822/wife-of-man-shot-by-mesa-police-seeks-help-from-hacker-group-anonymous

Anonymous Releases Details Of 52 Police Officers In Retaliation For Civilian Shooting -
http://www.mirror.co.uk/tech/anonymous-releases-details-52-police-7415832

Anonymous releases personal information of 52 Cincinnati police employees after officers shot and killed a black man armed with an airsoft gun -
http://www.dailymail.co.uk/news/article-3458631/Anonymous-releases-personal-information-52-Cincinnati-police-employees-officers-shot-killed-black-man-armed-airsoft-gun.html

Anonymous Hacker Group Declares War On CPD & Releases Officer Information -
http://www.fox19.com/story/31276928/anonymous-hacker-group-declares-war-on-cpd-releases-officer-information

Anonymous Releases Personal Info Of 52 CPD Officers -
http://www.cincinnati.com/story/news/2016/02/22/anonymous-releases-personal-info-52-cpd-officers/80722040/

Anonymous Leaks Data Of 52 Cincinnati Police Officers -
http://news.softpedia.com/news/anonymous-leaks-data-of-52-
cincinnati-police-officers-500801.shtml

Anonymous Hackers Target Cincinnati Police Department -
http://www.bizjournals.com/cincinnati/news/2016/02/22/anonymous-
hackers-target-cincinnati-police.html

Anonymous Hackers Post Home Address Of Miami Police Union
Chief Javier Ortiz -
http://www.miaminewtimes.com/news/anonymous-hackers-post-
home-address-of-miami-police-union-chief-javier-ortiz-8271484

Anonymous Threatens Cincinnati Police -
http://wwlp.com/2016/02/23/anonymous-threatens-cincinnati-police/

Anonymous Releases MPD Officers Personal Info -
http://www.montgomeryadvertiser.com/story/news/local/blogs/moonb
log/2016/03/04/anonymous-releases-mpd-officers-personal-
information/81325762/

Anonymous Ghost Squad's DDoS Attack Shuts Down KKK Website
https://www.hackread.com/anonymous-ghost-squad-ddos-on-kkk-
website/

KKK Website Shut Down By Anonymous Ghost Squad's DDoS
Attack -
https://www.techworm.net/2016/04/kkk-website-shut-anonymous-
ghost-squads-ddos-attack.html

Anonymous Unmasks Female KKK Leader As War Against Masked
Fascist Group Intensifies -
http://www.mirror.co.uk/tech/anonymous-unmasks-female-ku-klux-
7845350

How Anonymous Is Fighting White Supremacy Online -
http://www.huffingtonpost.com/entry/anonymous-shut-down-kkk-website_us_5720c204e4b0b49df6a9b333

Anonymous Leaks Identity Of Prominent Ku Klux Klan Member -
http://www.ibtimes.co.uk/anonymous-allegedly-leaks-identity-prominent-ku-klux-klan-member-1557160

Anonymous Declares 'Day Of Solidarity' With BLM To Protest Police
-
http://www.ibtimes.co.uk/anonymous-declares-day-solidarity-black-lives-matter-protest-police-brutality-1569983

Anonymous goes to war against police brutality in the US -
https://betanews.com/2016/07/13/anonymous-goes-to-war-against-police-brutality/

Treachery Most Foul: The Betrayal Of Operation Ferguson -
http://anonymousglobal.org/commanderx/blog/?p=72

James Daniel McIntyre ID'd as man shot by RCMP in Dawson Creek
http://www.cbc.ca/news/canada/british-columbia/james-daniel-mcintyre-id-d-as-man-shot-by-rcmp-in-dawson-creek-1.3160317

Police Shoot Protester Wearing Anonymous Mask Hacktivist' Group Vows To
Avenge His Death -
http://countercurrentnews.com/2015/07/police-protester-wearing-anonymous-mask/

RCMP Website Crashes After Anonymous Threatens Revenge -
http://www.timescolonist.com/news/b-c/rcmp-website-crashes-after-anonymous-threatens-revenge-1.2005592

Cops Kill Man In Guy Fawkes Mas Anonymous Vows to Avenge The Police
Killing -
http://thefreethoughtproject.com/anonymous-launches-opanondown-
vow-avenge-police-killing-anon-member/#cKMVbgDuTf6BBPyh.99

Anonymous Claims Attack On RCMP Websites In Response To Police
Shooting -
http://www.ctvnews.ca/canada/anonymous-claims-attack-on-rcmp-
websites-in-response-to-police-shooting-1.2476710

Anonymous Claims Responsibility For Downed RCMP Website -
http://www.lifeinquebec.com/anonymous-hacks-rcmp-website-20360/

RCMP National Website Goes Offline Anonymous Claims Responsibility -
http://www.torontosun.com/2015/07/19/rcmp-national-website-goes-
offline-anonymous-claims-responsibility

RCMP National Website Goes Offline Anonymous Claims Responsibility -
http://www.newsoptimist.ca/rcmp-national-website-goes-offline-
anonymous-claims-responsibility-1.2005660

Anonymous Claims Attack On RCMP Websites In Response To Dawson
Creek Shooting -
https://warriorpublications.wordpress.com/2015/07/19/anonymous-
claims-attack-on-rcmp-websites-in-response-to-dawson-creek-
shooting/

RCMP Website Back Online After Shutdown -
http://www.dawsoncreekmirror.ca/rcmp-website-back-online-after-
shutdown-1.2005582

Anonymous Warns Canada Police: There'll Be Revenge -
http://www.presstv.ir/Detail/2015/07/20/421083/Canada-police-
Anonymous-British-Colombia-Guy-Fawkes

RCMP National Website Goes Offline Anonymous Claims Responsibility -
http://globalnews.ca/news/2119716/rcmp-national-website-goes-offline-anonymous-claims-responsibility/

Anonymous Ramps Up Response To Deadly Police Shooting In Dawson Creek -
http://www.news1130.com/2015/07/20/anonymous-has-ramped-up-response-to-deadly-police-shooting-in-dawson-creek-analyst/

Anonymous Says It Will Release Name Of RCMP Officer Involved In Dawson Creek Shooting -
http://www.vancitybuzz.com/2015/07/anonymous-states-will-release-name-rcmp-officer-involved-dawson-creek-shooting/

Is Anonymous Becoming The Modern Day Technological Robin Hood? -
http://globalnews.ca/news/2120911/watch-is-anonymous-becoming-the-modern-day-technological-robin-hood/

Anonymous Targets Canadian Mounted Police After Shooting -
http://www.wsbradio.com/news/national/anonymous-targets-canadian-mounted-police-after-shooting/MNwt9x7IbcDqyNsYaJHkXN/

Anonymous Declares War Against Canadian Police And Launches Attacks -
http://www.inquisitr.com/2266576/anonymous-declares-war-against-canadian-police-launches-cyber-attacks/

Anonymous Hacktivists Threaten Canada With Leak Of Classified Info -
http://www.theepochtimes.com/n3/1599038-anonymous-hacktivists-threaten-canada-with-leak-of-classified-information/

RCMP Offline As Deadline Looms For Anonymous Leak Threat -
http://ipolitics.ca/2015/07/27/rcmp-offline-as-deadline-looms-for-anonymous-threat-to-expose-secret-documents/

Anonymous CSIS Document Leak Probed By RCMP & CSE -
http://www.cbc.ca/news/canada/anonymous-csis-document-leak-probed-by-rcmp-cse-1.3171099

Ottawa Says Little About CSIS Document Breach Claimed By Anonymous -
https://www.thestar.com/news/canada/2015/07/28/ottawa-says-little-about-csis-document-breach-claimed-by-anonymous.html

Anonymous Releases Hacked CSIS Document & Threatens To Leak Stunning Secrets -
http://news.nationalpost.com/news/canada/anonymous-releases-hacked-csis-document-threaten-to-leak-stunning-secrets-at-irregular-intervals

Anonymous Vows To Leak More Secret Federal Documents After Apparent Breach -
http://www.huffingtonpost.ca/2015/07/28/anonymous-canadian-government_n_7886656.html

Hackers Target Canadian Government Websites -
https://www.theglobeandmail.com/news/national/hackers-target-canadian-government-website/article25729750/

Tr1cK - Junaid Hussain - https://en.wikipedia.org/wiki/Junaid_Hussain

TeaMp0isoN - https://en.wikipedia.org/wiki/TeaMp0isoN

In Defense Of Online Protest: An Anon Goes On Hunger Strike To Protest The CFAA & Abusive Prosecutions -
http://anonymousglobal.org/commanderx/blog/?p=263

www.ingramcontent.com/pod-product-compliance
Lightning Source LLC
Chambersburg PA
CBHW031831170526
45157CB00001B/263